General Editor – Construction and Civil Engineering

C. R. Bassett, B.Sc.
Formerly Principal Lecturer in the Department of Building and Surveying, Guildford County College of Technology

Books already published in this sector of the series:

Building organisations and procedures   *G. Forster*
Construction site studies – production, administration and
   personnel   *G. Forster*
Practical construction science   *B. J. Smith*
Construction science Volume 1   *B. J. Smith*
Construction science Volume 2   *B. J. Smith*
Construction mathematics Volume 1   *M. K. Jones*
Construction mathematics Volume 2   *M. K. Jones*
Construction surveying   *G. A. Scott*
Materials and structures   *R. Whitlow*
Construction technology Volume 1   *R. Chudley*
Construction technology Volume 2   *R. Chudley*
Construction technology Volume 3   *R. Chudley*
Construction technology Volume 4   *R. Chudley*
Maintenance and adaptation of buildings   *R. Chudley*
Building services and equipment Volume 1   *F. Hall*
Building services and equipment Volume 2   *F. Hall*
Building services and equipment Volume 3   *F. Hall*
Measurement Level 2   *M. Gardner*
Structural analysis   *G. B. Vine*
Site surveying and levelling Level 2   *H. Rawlinson*
Economics for the construction industry   *R. C. Shutt*
Design procedures Level 4   *J. M. Zunde*
Environmental science   *B. J. Smith, M. E. Sweeney and G. M.
   Phillips*
Design procedures Level 2   *M. Barritt*

Contents

viii

Preface

For every member of the design team in building, including the architectural technician, theoretical studies in design run in parallel with increasing understanding of the technology both of construction and of the control of the environment.

Design Technology is a subject area in which the relevance of such studies to design is explored. It stresses the importance of sound technical knowledge if efficient use of available resources, to provide buildings which fulfil the needs of their users, is to be achieved.

This book has been prepared to cover the syllabus of TEC unit U77/441, Design Technology Level 5, which is part of the required programme for architectural technicians. It presupposes knowledge of technology to Level 4 and of Design Procedures to Level 2 of the TEC programme.

Starting from an initial survey of the major properties of the materials used in buildings, and the environmental functions buildings are expected to perform, it discusses specification writing and detailing, quality control, the diagnosis and treatment of faults, and factory production. There is also reference to the adaptation and maintenance requirements of buildings. The material is presented in a form likely to be convenient as a reference for designers and technicians concerned with many aspects of buildings, and as a textbook for students in these disciplines.

The author wishes to acknowledge the assistance of her colleagues, including particularly Chris Tipple, who read and commented constructively upon Chapters 6 and 14, and Gillian Hayes who helped similarly with Chapters 7 and 13. The unfailing help of Colin Bassett, General Editor, Building and Civil Engineering to the Longman Technician Series, whose continual support is greatly appreciated, and of all the friendly and considerate people at the publishers' office, must be mentioned. She must also record her thanks for the continued cheerful understanding of her daughters, Ingrid and Helga.

Joan Zunde
Sheffield
1981

Chapter 1

Introduction

Design is a logical process. The professional designer does not wait around for inspiration to strike, he must work to a timetable and justify the time he spends upon a problem. He knows that there is always more than one possible solution to a problem, and that he is most likely to discover the one best suited to the conditions by an ordered and rational approach. However simple or complex the task may be, applying the principles of 'creative problem-solving' is usually the most effective and efficient way to work.

The first step is the analysis of the problem so that the whole of the requirements and the environmental circumstances are fully understood. This involves the collection of all the relevant data, since the emergence at a later stage of some important but hitherto unrecognised requirement might undermine the whole of the work so far done.

Secondly, the priorities and other relationships between the various requirements are explored. Cost and quality, time and craftsmanship, the levels of the the site and a sprawling preferred plan arrangement could be pairs of interrelated conditions in the case of a building project where conflicts might need to be resolved before progress could be made. This process generally has the effect of throwing-up (in outline) a number of potential solutions to the whole problem.

In the next stage, two or more of the more promising of these ideas are developed, with constant evaluation of their success against the established criteria. Techniques such as lateral thinking and brainstorming may be applied, and it will eventually become clear which solution should be put forward to the client for consideration.

Finally, the recommended solution is presented to the client in drawings, models and written reports as may be suitable to the case.

Design Procedures is the subject which examines this approach in depth, and many students attempting Design Technology will have completed a fourth level course in that subject. Design Technology is concerned with the technical knowledge and skills required for Design Procedures to be effectively carried out.

In the context of building this is very largely based on an understanding of the materials that are available for use, the ways in which they are produced and can be used sensibly, and the mechanisms which may cause them (and the structures into which they are assembled) to deteriorate.

Technology

This is a term whose precise meaning has developed over the years. A comparison between up-to-date dictionaries shows some variation in the definitions given.

The *Oxford English Dictionary* says that it is derived from the Greek for a systematic treatment (of grammar, etc.), and goes on

1. A discourse or treatise on an art or arts, the scientific study of the practical or industrial arts.
2. Practical arts collectively. The terminology of a particular art or subject; technical nomenclature.

Webster has

1. The terminology of a particular subject: technical language.
2. The science of the application of knowledge to practical purposes: applied science.
3. The totality of the means employed by a people to provide itself with the objects of material culture.

Chambers (revised) says

1. The practice, description and terminology of any or all of the applied sciences which have practical value and/or industrial use;
2. technical method(s) in a particular field of industry or art;
3. technical means and skills characteristic of a particular civilisation, group or period.

All these definitions, from general dictionaries, are interesting. They do not seem (apart from Chambers 2) to agree with the way the word is used in ordinary speech, however ('The work force was on strike against the introduction of new technology') nor with the way the term is understood by technologists, which is much deeper.

The McGraw-Hill *Encyclopedia of Science and Technology* has, 'Systematic knowledge and action, usually of industrial processes but applicable to any recurrent activity.'

The Open University, in the 'Introduction' to the foundation course 'Living with Technology' develops a satisfying definition, as follows.

'Technology is the application of scientific and other organized [*sic*] knowledge to practical tasks by hierarchically ordered systems that involve people and machines.'

As you will see, McGraw-Hill introduce the idea of 'systematic action' while the Open University extends this to include the way in which a process is organised and the people involved. It is the Open University definition which I have adopted here.

Systems

This is another term which is often used loosely. Systems ideas are an integral part of technology, and the word needs to be correctly understood.

Correctly, a system is a collection of parts which work together to produce a result that would be impossible if they were not linked. The system has a boundary, within which the parts lie, and an environment which it affects. Anything whose removal would adversely affect the way the system works lies within the boundary – elements of the environment are affected by the system but do not in turn affect IT.

This apparently complicated idea actually helps considerably in understanding how elaborate organisations and processes work, and is easier to follow if one tries to see how the parts of some familiar system, such as a polytechnic or a motor car, fit into the definition. What are the parts of the system, and what is its environment? What are its aims, and how does it achieve them?

The important characteristic of a system referred to above, that it

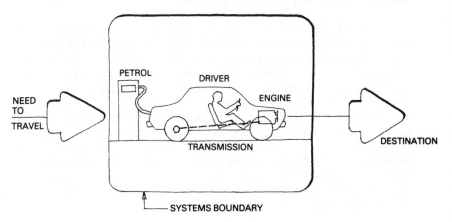

Fig. 1.1 A system

achieves something the parts individually could not have attained, is known as 'synergy'. The synergistic effect in the case of an educational institution is the interplay of minds, both among staff and students, and the economic use of shared facilities perhaps. A car is clearly immobilised if a vital part breaks down, so quite evidently synergy is displayed there. (See Fig. 1.1.)

Using the word system correctly, then, a systematic approach to design involves the application of all the parts of the process by an organised team of people who understand it thoroughly and who also have a sound grasp of the technology that will be employed to fulfil their intentions. The synergy of the system is displayed when the steps cease to be discrete operations and become a single generative process.

In Fig. 1.2 the boundaries, components and environment of such a system are suggested, together with its objectives.

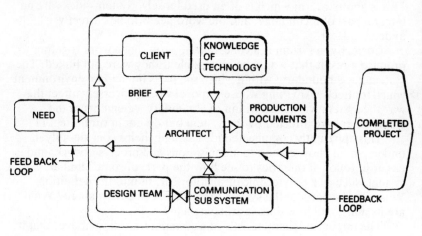

Fig. 1.2 Design may be seen as a system

Design Technology, too, can be conceived as a system. The components include factual information, people with the skill and knowledge to apply it and techniques (such as drawing or specification writing) which are employed. The environment of the system includes both the client and the builder. Each of these is affected by the conclusions of the process, but does not take part in it. It would be reasonable to take the view that the client is part of the 'design' system (since a change in his requirements will affect all that that system does) but not of the 'technology' system, while although the building **industry** is clearly an important part of the 'technology' system, the particular builder in most cases cannot be, since he has not usually been identified when the system is in operation. Figure 1.3 shows the 'technology' system.

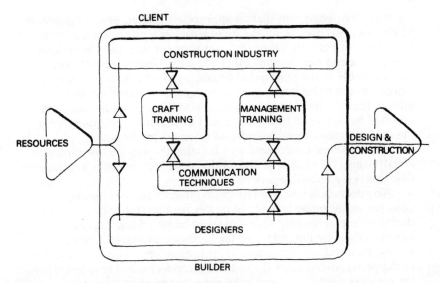

Fig. 1.3 The 'system' of design technology

Communication

One further, and very important, aspect of Design Technology is that it is generally necessary to communicate precise information of a technical kind to other parties during and at the end of the design period. If this is to be satisfactorily achieved, both communicator and recipient need to be aware of the basic theory of communication.

Figure 1.4 shows how a message is passed between two people.

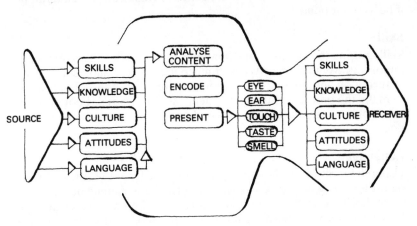

Fig. 1.4 Communication

It is, first, important that an appropriate carrier, or signal, should be chosen. This may be an electrical pulse, or a piece of paper with lines on it, or light, or paper with words on, or flags used in various ways, or indeed one of many other vehicles. Whatever is chosen, as being suitable to the material to be conveyed, the distance it has to travel, the use to be made of it by the recipient, and so on, the information will have to be translated into the applicable code, and decoded before it can be understood. For example, the originator of the message may choose to transmit information about the three-dimensional object such as a building through the medium of a line drawing. He has to use conventional symbols in order to achieve this: this is the encoding process.

Any distortion which enters during transmission or during encoding or decoding is liable to render the message unclear, and we therefore aim at limiting such unwanted 'noise'. Some may be introduced by the limitations of the hardware available (like the narrow bandwidth of telephone transmissions) but a good deal is due to the personal 'filters' of the individuals concerned. These filters are the result of the background, education and so on of everyone, through which we try to communicate with the world. They limit our ability to express our meaning and to comprehend the meaning of others, and five separate elements are identifiable. The closer the 'match' of originator and recipient on these points, the better their chance of effective communication.

Knowledge

Most messages presuppose some background of general information. If this turns out not to exist, serious misunderstanding could result. It's no use telling a man which coloured wire to connect to which terminal if he's colour blind.

Skill

Skill in using the channels of communication at both ends is obviously important. My radio receiver isn't much use unless I understand how to turn it on and tune it. We have to acquire skills of this kind if we are to make the best use of the many media at our disposal. Poor drawing or scribble or inept speech is a second important source of distorting noise.

Language

Using the tools is not the same as grasping the language (the code) to be used. It may be perfectly easy to master the technique of semaphoring with flags, but much more difficult to remember the sign for each letter and the conventions usually adopted. It is obviously useless to address a monoglot Russian in Chinese – it may not be quite so obvious that someone else's understanding of one's specialised technical language is deficient. This introductory chapter may possibly contain words outside the reader's vocabulary. If he is wise, he reads with a dictionary to hand, rather than try to guess the meaning from the context, since the recipient of a message has a duty to be aware of the possibility of noise, and guard against it, as well as the originator.

Attitude

A speaker who passionately advocates vegetarianism will find it hard to get a serious (let alone a sympathetic) hearing if he finds he has blundered by mistake into a convention of butchers. A similar difficulty could, to a lesser degree, face a Brutalist trying to explain his philosophy to plasterers. Since we all have prejudices, whether we like to admit it or not, we should always try to attend carefully to messages to which we are unsympathetic, for these are the ones we are most likely to misinterpret.

Anyone who talks down to, or is in awe of, the person on the other end of the communication line is likely to exacerbate this difficulty.

Culture

Much of our understanding of new material depends on our ability to relate it to what is familiar. This varies with the cultural background, and so where this is poorly understood many misconstructions may arise. Where there is clearly an ethnic or a generation gap we generally make automatic allowances for this: we may not do so where the distinction is the subtler one between the inner-city sophisticate and the advocate of the simple country life, between the master tailor and the high street clothier, or between the local authority housing manager and the speculative house-builder.

All of this might appear to mean that one can only communicate effectively with one's twin, which is not, of course, the case. What it in fact means is that we need to be aware of all the factors which might hinder the perfect reception of the information by introducing distorting noise into the communication system. Each must try to understand the context in which the other speaks or hears as far as possible. A good teacher begins from what she knows are the familiar experiences of her class, relating the new facts she has to teach to what is familiar so that it will quickly and easily be assimilated. When a child tries to explain some (to him) new phenomenon to her she expects he will do so in terms of his everyday experience.

As both originators and recipients of messages, designers would find intelligibility improved if they applied equal empathy.

Quality

One further definition which ought to be set out is that of 'quality'.

This abstract word is used in this book in two ways. Firstly, and most importantly it refers to the standard of workmanship or materials which will be acceptable in particular circumstances. This is defined by the specification (see Ch. 5) and ensured by the process of quality control described in Chapter 6. It is not to be taken as some absolute standard of excellence, nor the best level which can possible be achieved. The quality required has to be set out carefully and clearly understood by everyone concerned.

Secondly, 'quality' is used as a synonym of a characteristic (of a particular material or assembly) without overtones of value judgement. I believe it is clear from the context which sense the word carries, wherever it appears.

Design Technology, then, is a system. Its objective is the efficient application of the armoury of available technical resources to the solution of design problems and the definition and attainment of suitable standards of quality. The components of the system include factual information, techniques and people skilled in their use, and who display the synergy of acting as a team. The systems environment includes the client whose needs are being defined and met and the builder who carries out the designers' intentions. The study of Design Technology includes the practice of skills, the acquisition of knowledge, and the development of attitudes.

The boundary between Design Technology and Design Procedures is, as will be well understood from this chapter, amorphous. The detailed areas overlap. Students will be well advised to regard this subject as an extension of their previous excursions into the realm of design, and not as an unconnected ramble.

Chapter 2

Materials

The very wide range of materials available for use in building includes some which have been in common use for many centuries, and of which, therefore, there is a wide and detailed experience, and others introduced only in very recent years.

Primitive man commonly uses the materials he finds at hand and develops the techniques with which to make the best use of them, while he comes to understand their characteristics and capabilities to an almost instinctive extent. Such intimate experience of the whole range of materials available to modern builders is impractical, and study is needed if mistakes are to be avoided. Every material ought to be selected and used in the full knowledge of its characteristics and capabilities. These should be exploited as fully as possible, while the material's limitations are recognised and it is not expected to perform beyond them.

This chapter tries to summarise the major qualities of some of the commonest building materials. It will frequently be essential to consult manufacturers and research data when contemplating the specification of a new application, or a familiar one in rather extreme conditions.

Bricks and brickwork

The history of bricks can be traced back some 9 000 years, so this is the earliest case of a fabricated building material. As long ago as 1571, a Charter laid down a standard size, in inches, of $9 \times 4\frac{1}{4} \times 2\frac{1}{4}$ for bricks, so establishing one of the first areas of dimensional coordination. This size, based on weight, flexibility in the use of brickwork and economy, has hardly changed to the present day. For many years, bricks had a nominal size, in inches, of $9 \times 4\frac{1}{2} \times 3$, which after allowing for $\frac{3}{8}$ in. joints gave actual sizes of $8\frac{5}{8} \times 4\frac{1}{8} \times 2\frac{5}{8}$, and there was also a thinner size. On metrication, the designated size, in millimetres, of $225 \times 112.5 \times 75$ of BS 3921 gives actual sizes of $215 \times 102.5 \times 65$ allowing 10 mm for joints. There are made, however, other so-called 'metric' bricks nominally $300 \times 100 \times 100$ or 75 and $200 \times 100 \times 100$ or 75, to suit 'preferred dimensions' and there have been cases of confusion as to which of these various 'standards' is intended.

Bricks consist essentially of clay burnt at high temperature to produce a material of high compressive strength. The variations between different types depend partly on the clay from which they are made – which in particular affects their colour and strength – and partly on the method of manufacture, which has more influence on appearance.

Pressed or moulded bricks

About two-thirds of the bricks produced in this country are pressed. They are strongly compressed in moulds, and can be recognised by the depression, or frog, in one bed. This has the dual effect of lightening the brick and of providing some key for the mortar. (See Fig. 2.1.) Pressed bricks are reasonably accurate in shape and have crisp arrises.

Wire-cut bricks

Most of the remaining clay bricks are of this type. Clay is extruded in a continuous stream and cut into slices of the correct thickness by wires. They can be, and often are, made with holes through them which reduce the weight considerably below that of a pressed brick and also provide a better mortar key. They are efficient to dry and fire because of the greater area of exposed surface, and it seems likely that their advantages will lead to them forming an increasing proportion of production. (See Fig. 2.1.)

Hand-made bricks

Hand-made bricks are relatively rare and expensive, but have unrivalled subtlety of texture and colour. They usually have no frog, and never have holes, and the delivery is likely to include a wider variation in size and irregularity than would generally be acceptable in machine-made bricks. (See Fig. 2.1.)

Facing bricks

Facings are bricks manufactured and selected for their appearance, colour, texture and regularity all being important. Many have a common body with a surface finish applied by sand or a thin, bonded

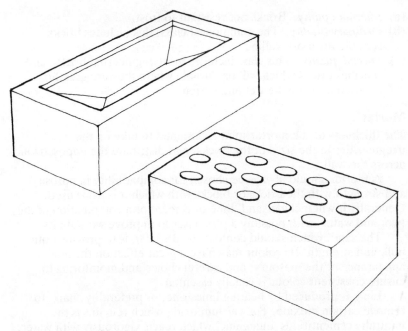

Fig. 2.1 Frog or perforations lighten the brick and provide a key

layer of coloured clay, while others are textured by sand or by mechanical means. The available range is very wide.

Calcium silicate bricks

These unburnt bricks are very precise in shape and colour, texture and strength. The wide range of colours includes some very pale ones, and they are often chosen on grounds of appearance.

Concrete bricks

These are available, but not in very widespread use.

Engineering bricks

These bricks have a body of great and known strength, and may fall into either of two classes, sometimes referred to as semi-engineering and engineering, but more correctly as classes A and B. Brindles and blue engineering bricks have a precise, machine-made character which sometimes leads to their selection where strength is unimportant. Engineering bricks are also resistant to water, and can be used in damp proof courses (DPC)s.

Quality

Common, facing and engineering bricks may all vary in quality.

(a) *Internal quality*. Bricks not resistant to frost.
(b) *Ordinary quality*. The commonest class, this includes bricks suitable for most walling.
(c) *Special quality*. This class includes most engineering bricks, and specifies bricks which will be durable where they are greatly exposed and may be wet and frozen.

Mortar

The thickness of the mortar joint is designed to take up the irregularities in the sizes of the bricks, and distribute the imposed loads across the wall.

A mortar should always be chosen for compatibility in porosity and strength with the bricks or blocks with which it is to be used. Generally it will include sand, lime or cement or a combination of the two, and water, with possibly a plasticiser to improve workability.

The sand, which should conform to BS 1200, is to provide both bulk and strength. Its colour may have a great effect on the final appearance of the masonry, and careful choice and monitoring to ensure consistent colour is usually essential.

Lime is produced by heating limestone, or preferably chalk, to remove carbon dioxide. The calcium oxide which remains is the naturally cementitious 'quicklime' which reacts vigorously with water, releasing heat to produce slaked lime. This, when exposed becomes calcium carbonate and sets. As slaked lime cannot be stored, lime is usually delivered in a powdered form which has been water-treated, 'hydrated lime'. Overburnt lime is hard to slake, and it should be noted that quicklime is dangerous and can burn.

Portland cement is a burnt mixture of two parts of chalk to one part of clay heated to about 1 400 °C, to which, when ground to powder a small proportion of gypsum is added to retard the set.

Cement alone as a hardening agent produces too strong a mortar for most purposes, and a proportion of lime is generally incorporated to improve workability and adhesion. The general rule is to use a proportion of one part of cementitious material to three parts of sand. A mix of 1 : 2 : 9 of cement to lime to sand is a good general-purpose mortar for external walls. The proportion of cement is increased relative to the lime for exposed conditions and may be decreased where strength is not critical.

The water used in mortar must be clean, water fit for drinking normally being considered suitable.

All the materials need to be accurately batched by volume, and allowance must be made for any water content of the sand.

The materials must be mixed dry before water is added and the mortar used directly it is mixed. Mortar which has begun to set cannot be 'knocked-up' for re-use, and has to be discarded, so only the quantities actually required should be made at any time.

Good brickwork is accurate in level and verticality, the perpends lie accurately above one another, and cut bricks are avoided except where they are demanded by the bond. All joints are completely filled with mortar, while cavities are kept clear of mortar droppings and mortar stains on the face are entirely avoided.

Flemish and English bond and their variations are little in evidence nowadays because cavity walls are in such widespread use. Where they are used they should be correctly carried out not only in the interests of appearance but also in those of strength.

Defects

Efflorescence
Salts contained in the bricks or mortar of a wall may be washed out by rain and deposited on the surface as a harmless but unsightly white powder, which can be washed off but should not be sealed.

Sulphate attack
Sulphates may attack the tricalcium aluminate in Portland cement, causing softening and disintegration. The sulphate content of bricks to be used in particularly wet conditions should be limited for this reason.

Frost damage
Water held in the porous structure of bricks without expansion space results in mechanical damage on freezing, entire faces in some instances spalling off. The selection of bricks known from experience to resist frost attack is essential for external use, and especially for brick-on-edge copings.

Underburnt bricks have suspect durability and strength. They are recognised by colour and hardness, and should be rejected.

Bricks have outstandingly good fire resistance, having already been fired to temperatures well in excess to those reached in building fires.

Character
Brick is often thought of as a soft, gentle and sympathetic material to use, which blends easily into a landscape. While this may have been true of, say, the cottages of East Anglia, where handmade bricks of the local clay, well weathered by exposure, integrate well with their surroundings, it is not universally true. A visit to any of the many brick-built housing developments will show that this can be a hard and brash material, particularly where colour and texture are selected to provide restless variety.

The very precise use of gauged brickwork in the Low Countries, and increasingly here, may indicate a more fruitful approach to the use of the material. Modern bricks are mostly hard and machine-made, they can have precisely controlled colour and texture, which does not need to mimic that of the hand-made product, and they are well adapted to be used almost like faience. It was the inherent

Fig. 2.2 Crisp detail can characterise brickwork

irregularities of older bricks which resulted in the informality of the effect they produced. (See Fig. 2.2.)

Concrete

The four major constituents of concrete, which is a material that has been in use since the time of the Romans, are fine aggregate – commonly sand, coarse aggregate – gravel or stone particles of a specified size range, a binding agent which is most commonly Portland cement, and water. All need to be clean and free from organic matter.

Workability
Well-graded aggregate produces the most workable concrete, though air entrainers can be incorporated to improve this characteristic. The slump test gives a site measure of workability, though more accurate tests are available.

Additives
Besides workability agents, additives may be incorporated in the mix to accelerate setting, or to waterproof the concrete. These last are

somewhat suspect, as it is impossible to ensure that they have been fully dispersed through the mix: they have the effect, however, of calling attention to the need for accurate batching and adequate mixing, which may in itself lead to greater density and hence water resistance in the concrete.

Strength

To ensure that the design strength of concrete is being achieved, the taking and testing of test cubes is essential. The time lag before results are available may make the removal of concrete which proves to be below standard expensive and inconvenient, and sometimes the addition of extra members is preferred. However, the knowledge that regular tests are being carried out has a salutary effect on workmanship.

Cement

(See also the remarks under 'Bricks and brickwork: mortar' above.)

A variety of cements is available for use where rapid hardening or resistance to sulphate attack or other particular qualities are required. Careful storage of cement in dry conditions is essential to preserve its quality.

Water–cement ratio

Water is necessary to activate the cement, but the water–cement ratio is highly significant. Any water beyond what is needed for that purpose will result in voids in the concrete, with loss of strength. However, too dry a mix will be difficult to mix and to pack properly around reinforcement. Vibration assists workability of a dry mix.

Concrete has good fire-resistance, so it is often chosen to encase steelwork, and it has excellent compressive, though practically no tensile, strength.

While the cement acts as a setting agent, a mix consisting entirely of cement and water would be hard, brittle and expensive. Aggregate provides bulk and is cheaper than cement. It is also more resistant to cracking and shrinkage, and its inclusion minimises the movement and consequent damage that might otherwise occur.

It is important that the aggregate should have a compressive strength equal to that of the cement/sand with which it is incorporated, but the use of stronger aggregate, such as granite chippings, is unlikely in itself to improve the strength of the concrete.

Mixes

Design of a mix has to take into account:
(a) The size of the members and the spacing of any reinforcement (which will limit the maximum size of aggregate).
(b) The 'sharpness' of the aggregate, which affects workability.
(c) The strength required.

(d) The plant available and the level of supervision.

Ready-mix concrete, whose strength is notably well controlled, is now widely used in preference to site-mixing. This makes tighter design feasible.

Reinforced concrete (RC)

In this material, concrete is assumed to carry the whole of the compressive stresses, while steel is introduced to deal with the tension. The steel is well protected from damp and from fire by the concrete, providing no hair cracks are allowed to develop.

The pre- or post-stressing of RC allows much finer members to be designed, as well as reducing the overall mass, because initial compression is applied to the concrete to allow for a similar degree of tension to be applied later during use.

The design of shell and lattice structures has reached a level of sophistication which permits great economy and elegance of form, provided that the building is allowed to take the optimum configuration demanded by the structure. Any attempt to torture the structure into shapes other than those demanded by the calculations seems to be doomed to failure.

Defects

The commonest defect in concrete is spalling of cover from RC members. This may be due in part to poor adhesion between the concrete and the reinforcement (twisted reinforcement and the hooking of bar ends both aid adhesion) but is more likely to be due to water having entered through hair cracks, leading to expansion due to rusting of the steel.

Concrete which is over-worked after placement develops excessive 'laitence' due to cement slurry rising to the surface. Applied finishes which adhere to laitence rather than to the body of the concrete are liable to fail.

Concrete is widely considered to be a harsh and unsympathetic material, which is best hidden by applied finishes. These are most successful aesthetically where they are chosen to express the rugged nature of the concrete, and certainly where there is no attempt to ape other methods of construction, such as masonry. Unfortunately the adhesion of some such finishes has proved less than perfect on occasion, with results generally agreed to be even less pleasing than the naked concrete.

A preferable expedient may be to control the mix, placing and shuttering so that the concrete itself provides a homogeneous and pleasing appearance: this has proved satisfactory in a number of instances. The character evoked is masculine and strong, and is well suited to massive and monumental structures.

An alternative is the integral finish applied during casting rather than subsequently, or the working of the surface after the shuttering is struck, for example by bush hammering.

In the case of delicate members, the fineness of the necessary mix is usually sufficient to ensure an acceptable appearance without the need for an applied finish.

Timber

Timber was one of the earliest materials to come into use in building, and for many centuries it was used lavishly in structural members, joinery and finishings without regard to economy. Structural members in buildings still standing from the Middle Ages may be found to be riddled with the tunnels made by the larvae of woodboring insects and yet retain adequate strength because of the redundant material originally provided.

Although timber is a renewable resource, it is being used at a greater rate than it is produced, and we must today be more provident in its use. We have the knowledge on which proper grading can be based, and which allows accurate design. The need to minimise sizes so as to minimise weights imposed on other members is also recognised.

It is now usual for softwoods to be employed for the vast majority of structural purposes, while hardwoods are used – apart from a few exposed situations, such as cills – almost exclusively where their superior colour or figure is to be exploited.

Structure

Timber, which is usually slightly acid, consists largely of cellulose, with some hemicellulose and lignin (which is the bonding agent) and resins and other minor constituents. These trace elements may be important in practice, and if they are known to be present the advice of manufacturers of adhesives and paints should be sought before their products are used.

The outermost layer, below the bark, of a tree is the cambium, or sapwood, which is the growing part of the organism, subdividing to add new cells. Softwood has a system of longitudinal cells called tracheids which are cross-linked by a tissue known as parenchyma which is mainly a store for the sugar or starch of the plant food. The tracheids may be thought of as a bundle of tubes through which nourishment is distributed. Salts from the soil rise in solution, and the leaves draw carbon dioxide from the air and, with the sunlight for fuel, these react with the chlorophyll in the leaves to produce starch. When the sap is rising in spring and early summer the tree grows rapidly and large fibres are added, while smaller ones are made as growth slows later in the year. This accounts for the familiar rings seen in a cross-section of a tree. The entire structure is known as the xylem. Because trees are

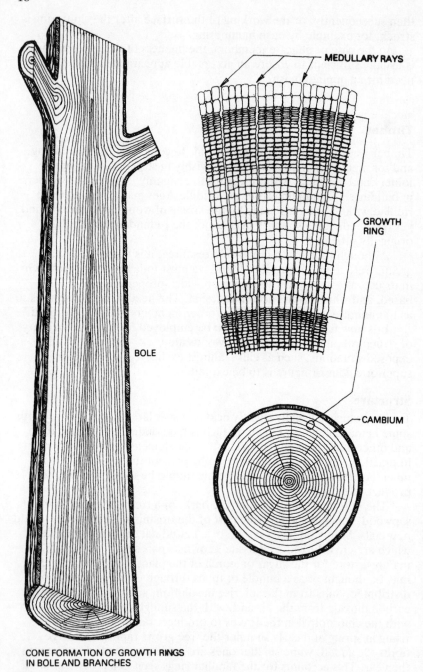

MEDULLARY RAYS

GROWTH RING

CAMBIUM

BOLE

CONE FORMATION OF GROWTH RINGS
IN BOLE AND BRANCHES

Fig. 2.3 The structure of timber

directly responsive in their growth to weather conditions, archeologists claim accurate dating of timber samples by comparison of the xylem with examples of known date. (See Fig. 2.3.)

The sapwood feeds to some extent, in a mature tree, on residual food material stored in the heartwood, which is for this reason more resistant to insect attack. The fibres of the heartwood are generally blocked with tissue.

While softwoods are almost invariably the timber of fast-growing conifers, hardwoods come from flowering plants, generally deciduous. They have thick-walled fibres and usually a denser texture.

It is usual to describe the material used in carpentry – the structural parts of the building – as timber, while that used in joinery is referred to as wood.

Defects

Because it is a natural material, wood varies considerably in its texture, and is liable to show the effects of irregular growth or attack by pests during the life of the tree. Many such defects are of little structural significance, though they may be unsightly. The principal ones include the following.

Knots

These occur where a branch or twig has joined the main stem, diverting the pattern of the xylem. If they are dead or loose they should be cut out and replaced by plugs, so long as this will not show. Where the wood is to be visible, the section should be rejected if it contains dead or loose knots. Live knots have a limited effect on tensile strength, but are usually acceptable. BS 1186 limits the number and size of knots acceptable in structural members and forbids the use of any timber containing dead knots in joinery or surfaces to be stained.

Shakes and splits

There is some confusion in the use of these terms, both of which denote fissures in the wood. It is correct to refer to those parallel to the rings as shakes and to radial fissures as splits. Neither is acceptable in joinery and only small gaps can be accepted in structural timbers.

Dote and punk

Dote is a fungal decay which causes white patches and streaks which need not be rejected so long as they will not be seen. Punk is an associated softening of the fibrous structure, and must be rejected.

Moisture content

All timber contains moisture, and any exposed surface will begin to dry out. It is therefore clearly desirable to complete the necessary drying before wood comes to be worked, and seasoning aims to reduce the moisture content throughout the piece to a level equivalent to that in which the timber is to be used, since drying is inevitably accompanied by shrinkage. Since timber is also hydroscopic, it takes up moisture from a damp atmosphere, and will tend to reach equilibrium with the humidity of the air unless it is protected, so care is needed if the stability of the material is to be properly protected from conversion to use. The drying is done by seasoning – generally nowadays in a steady temperature in a kiln. Seasoning does nothing to preserve timber, and indeed the modern rapid methods sometimes mean that dormant insect attack goes undetected. All structural timbers ought really to be protected by pressure impregnation with a recognised preservative as a safeguard against decay.

Conversion

Since the drying shrinkage of timber varies with the direction of the face relative to the grain, twisting and warping can often occur. The shrinkage radially is about half that on the tangential surface, and there is negligible movement in the longitudinal direction. Radially-sawn timber is thus the most stable and methods of conversion such as 'quarter sawn' aim to utilise the maximum material with optimum shrinkage characteristics.

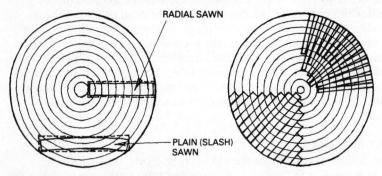

Fig. 2.4 The conversion of timber

Strength

Timber is strong in both tension and compression and has a high modulus of elasticity with good recovery characteristics. CP 112 schedules the structural properties of various groups of species and includes definitions of defects which may be acceptable in various circumstances.

Laminated boards and chipboard

These materials utilise timber which might otherwise be discarded because of its defects. Their properties are largely determined by the adhesives used.

Biological attack on timber in buildings is covered in Chapter 12.

Character

Because they provide long, even, lengths with straight grain, softwoods are admirably suited to structural uses. They are also commonly used in joinery for painting, because they can achieve a fine smooth finish superior to that which can be obtained from most hardwoods, whose irregularity of grain is hard to conceal. Their uniformity sometimes qualifies them, too, for visible use, suitably stained and varnished.

Softwood is sometimes deliberately left in a rough condition for effect, and this can be most successful, provided the roughness is genuine. 'Waney-edged boarding' and the like, produced by machine, is rarely successful.

Hardwood should be chosen, converted and used to exploit to the full the colour and grain which characterise it, otherwise the money spent – except in the case of oak cills and a few other instances – will have been wasted. Veneering allows the maximum use to be made of a beautiful configuration, and for it to be used repetitively. This process was so popular in the 1930s that it now has a period character, but it may be due for a revival.

It should be noted that what is considered a 'beautiful' figure has varied very much over the years, and that climbing on to the latest fashionable bandwagon is a sure way of 'dating' one's work.

Georgian Architects used hardwood for joinery, achieving much more delicate mouldings and especially astragals (glazing bars) than we should aspire to today. This perhaps was because they could be very selective in their choice of timber. Their mouldings were of a delicate subtlety difficult to match with machines. We might learn from them that there is a case for using fine hardwoods selectively where their qualities will be used to the full, and combining these with other more robust materials elsewhere.

Stone

Stone, or rock to the geologist, is a naturally occurring material of some abundance, great variety and uneven utility. It has been in use from the earliest times, at first in an undressed state as found, and later in a fine ashlar for ribbed structures. Latterly it has been much used as a facing.

Rocks are normally classified under three headings as follows.

Igneous

These stones, of which granite is a good example, were formed by the cooling of the magma, the molten material of the earth's core, and have a crystalline structure which varies with the rate of cooling which formed them. There is no bed. Granite has high chemical resistance and compressive strength. Though it is hard to work it will take a high polish which resists weathering. There is a wide range of colours including black, grey, grey-green and pink. It is expensive and is used for contrasted purposes in engineering and for monumental structures. Igneous rocks have a high silica content.

Sedimentary

Sedimentary rocks were formed by the compaction of sediment washed down by rivers or from shells and other animal debris. They show parallel layers or strata.

Sandstones are the result of the compaction of sand which is itself uncompacted mineral grains produced by the erosion of igneous rocks. They consist largely of quartz particles bound by a natural cement. They should be laid on the natural bed, as otherwise they may laminate under load or by the action of frost, and they are also liable to be damaged by water washing on to them off limestone. York stone is a typical sandstone.

Limestones consist largely of calcium carbonate in the form of calcite, at its purest in chalk. They result largely from the beds of old lakes, and some limestones (oolitic) contain 'roestones' formed by deposits of calcite around fragments of shell. The hardness of limestones varies and many are self-cleaning because they are slightly soluble in rainwater. Limestones generally improve in appearance when weathered. They must be correctly bedded. Bath and Portland stones are typical.

Metamorphic

These stones, which include marble, were changed by the action of pressure and heat, and (for example) marble is a metamorphic limestone.

They have a fine, crystalline structure, and polish well and can be delicately carved. They come in a range of colours and figures to suit almost any application. Though they are resistant to abrasion they lose their polish rapidly in acid-polluted conditions and are easily stained where it is damp.

Character

Stone masonry can produce virtually any effect from the crude monolith to gothic tracery, depending on careful selection of the stone and thoughtful detailing.

It is, perhaps, the most natural of materials, and certainly it is one of those of which we have the greatest wealth of knowledge and experience. Its variety of texture and colour is wide.

Random or coursed rubble have an informal and rural air which is unsuited to a town, while dressed ashlar is essentially urban and monumental in character. Granite and marble both have personalities so strong as to dominate any design of which they are major constituents.

Large units used in trabeated construction create an impression far removed from that of the small units which make up a medieval vault.

Some stones can be carved more easily than others and the choice should be made accordingly. It would generally be advocated that igneous stones should be left polished or show their naturally rugged character, but the magically textured surface of a church at Launceston, where practically every granite unit in the exterior is richly carved, gives one pause. There is, of course, always a case where a broken rule leads to success. Such occasional serendipities do not, however, invalidate a general rule.

Slate

Slate is a metamorphic clay, which cleaves easily into flat sheets and is eminently suited for roofing, paving and claddings. It is a particularly durable material, with outstanding chemical resistance, and strong – even, to some extent, in tension, so that it can be hung. It is stable.

Slate, however, which has a content of sulphide of iron, decays rapidly in damp conditions, but otherwise is virtually impervious to water, to the extent of being suitable for use in DPCs.

The range of colours available is wider than is sometimes supposed, including greys, purples and greens, and the colour can be darkened by polishing or waxing.

As used for roofing in industrial areas, slate has acquired a mean, drab character. It is, however, capable of creating an impression of cool, crisp accuracy that is well adapted to a hipped or mansard roof. The colour should be selected to harmonise with the walling.

Ridge tiles are sometimes used with slated roofs, but such an application needs care if the result is to be convincing.

It is generally suggested that slates are most suitably used over stone or rendered walls, tiles being used with bricks. The thicker green slates of Cumbria are akin to stone roofing, and look well over random and coursed rubble walls.

Steel

Steels are alloys of iron, formulated for improved strength, reliability and, particularly, elasticity. Much of the process is concerned with the removal of impurities from the pig iron. Iron ore is smelted with coke in a blast furnace to produce the pig, and a Bessemer converter makes steel directly from molten iron by using air to drive out the impurities, while more modern converters employ pure oxygen instead of air. Open-hearth and electric arc-furnaces are also used. The art of steelmaking is to remove natural impurities while carefully controlling the added ingredients so that a material of known properties is produced.

Most structural steels are 'mild' steels, though steels of higher and lower carbon content are available for wire and for forgings respectively. The addition of carbon improves tensile strength, which is further enhanced by heat treatment.

The mild-steel sections most used in building are hot-rolled to accurate shape, and their strength and other characteristics are known within fine limits.

Steel loses strength rapidly in fire, and must therefore usually be protected with fire-resisting material. It is subject to destructive oxidation, or rust, though 'weathering' steels, which are suitable for unprotected outdoor use because their oxidation produces a protective coating, are obtainable.

Steel may be bolted, riveted or welded.

Character

The protection of steel from the action of the weather may be by painting, bonding of a plastic coating, or galvanising. This last has a mottled grey appearance which is generally disliked, though it may be due for a return to fashionable favour. Bonded plastic coatings provide the most permanent protection – care has to be taken in selecting the colour, and this sometimes leads to timidity.

Steel frames may produce the most delicate of tracery, which can be exploited as the tracery of the lierne vault was. Such delicacy has much to commend it as a contrast to the masculine robustness of many modern structures.

Aluminium

Aluminium is an abundant element (Al) which makes up 7 per cent of the earth's crust. Because, however, it is hard to extract it has only come into use comparatively recently.

It is extracted from bauxite, by dissolving this in hot caustic soda to produce aluminium oxide. This, with the addition of cryolite, is heated to 1 000 °C and electrically split into aluminium and oxygen. It is a malleable and easily worked metal, it is light in weight and has high electrical and thermal conductivity but the disadvantage of being liable to severe thermal movement.

Aluminium is generally used in alloys formulated specially for particular purposes, such as structures, windows and door furniture. Alloys with tensile strength equal to that of steel are obtainable, but they suffer from a low modulus of elasticity. Deflection is liable to be high and this limits its use in structures, where it may cause unacceptable damage to finishes.

One great advantage of the light weight of aluminium is the minimising of imposed loads on supporting structures.

Aluminium may be cast or wrought, and components are often bolted though they can be welded or bonded with adhesives.

It is necessary to protect aluminium from attack by the alkalis in wet Portland cement, and so windows cannot be built into brickwork as it rises. Acids may also cause damage, making the metal unsuitable for use in plumbing.

The protection of aluminium by oxidation, which may occur naturally on exposure, is often accelerated by 'anodising'. The aluminium is used as an anode in the electrolysis of dilute sulphuric acid. Oxygen is produced at the anode, which reacts with the aluminium – producing a durable coating of aluminium oxide. The oxide can be coloured by adding dye to the electrolyte.

Character

Aluminium was once thought of as a precious metal, and the Shaftsbury memorial (Eros) in Piccadilly Circus was cast from it. Today it is particularly valued for its light weight. The colour of naturally oxidised aluminium is not greatly admired, and many designers prefer to paint it.

As a cladding material, aluminium presents a well-finished weather resistant face, and crisp moulding or pressed corrugations can be obtained.

Copper

The element copper (Cu) is ductile and an excellent electrical conductor. In its production, the ore is roasted to remove the sulphur, treated in a Bessemer converter and further refined by furnace or electrolytic treatment or both. Copper oxidises only slowly, becoming darker, but it is protected by a naturally formed patina of copper carbonate (verdigris) which has a usually admired soft green colour.

Green stains made by water washing off copper on to adjacent materials often occur, and these are both unsightly and difficult to remove. The resistance to corrosion of copper is high, though it can be attacked by water containing a high level of free carbon dioxide. Cold working improves the strength of the metal.

Copper is alloyed with tin to make bronze and with zinc to make brass, and such alloys can have excellent hardness, durability and workability. They are liable to darken in air.

Lead

The ductile element (Pb) is highly malleable, and also extremely poisonous. It is attacked by organic acids but protected by lead carbonate which forms a film on the surface during weathering. It is produced from the ore by sintering, or roasting, followed by reduction in a blast furnace and refinement. It is refined by being melted at low temperature in a reverbertory furnace.

Lead is expensive, and its use is normally confined today to applications where the ease with which it can be worked is important, such as flashings.

Metal corrosion

Metal corrosion is due to a chemical reaction between materials, often in the presence of oxygen or water or both. Salt water and the atmosphere alone may provide conditions for the effect, which in some cases produces a coating which covers the body and protects it from further attack, in the form of an oxide, salt or sulphide.

Some mystery surrounds the precise mechanism involved, but it is generally suggested that metal corrosion is due to electrolytic action between dissimilar metals, especially in the presence of damp and pollution, and in higher temperatures. Ions pass from the anode (that is, the baser metal, such as aluminium) to the cathode (the noble metal, such as copper) through the electrolytic medium of acid water, leaving a deposit of the anode on the cathode as in electro-plating, while the anode is corroded. Dissimilar metals should be separated by the positive barrier of an electrical insulator, especially where damp conditions can be anticipated.

Corrosion can also occur in the presence of the alkalis from Portland cement, and in sulphate-bearing soil bacteria may attack and soften cast iron.

Plastics

Although the plastics industry has been around for many decades, it is only since the Second World War that the use of man-made materials based on polymers has become general in building.

These are organic compounds, of high molecular weight, which are insoluble in water, solid at ordinary temperatures, and can be moulded. Their origin can in fact be traced back to the invention of the vulcanisation of rubber in 1842, which was followed in 1865 by the first recognisable plastic material, celluloid, which is said to have been developed as a substitute for ivory for billiard balls.

Most plastics are compounds of carbon with hydrogen, oxygen, nitrogen and chlorine, and the industry is heavily based on oil. In silicones, some carbon atoms are replaced by silicon, while in fluoroplastic hydrogen is replaced by fluorine.

In structure, plastics are long chains of atoms with side attachments which tangle together to form solids, and a very great variety of formulations to suit different applications is available.

The major classification of plastics is between:

(a) Thermoplastic plastics, which harden and soften with changes of temperature indefinitely; and

(b) Thermosetting plastics, which are often very complex chemically, and which, once they are fabricated, retain their form through subsequent applications of heat.

Copolymers are produced when two monomers are polymerised together.

Plastics can now serve almost any building purpose, and are widely used in DPCs and damp proof membranes (DPM)s, in floor, wall and ceiling finishes, as bonders and in claddings. They generally have a favourable strength – weight ratio, though they are frequently brittle. Grades for hot and cold situations, flexible or rigid ones, formulations for moulding or ones for flat fabrication can be had. Industry frequently has a specially developed plastic produced for any new use, and the possible applications seem endless.

Character

Plastics are losing the reputation for being 'cheap and nasty' that they once had, though they still display an unfortunate tendency to mimic the appearance of natural materials. Because of their inherent regularity, they fail in this aim, and appear artificial and unconvincing.

It is generally more satisfactory if we exploit the clear colours and uniformity of texture which are their strong points, use their amazing versatility to the full, and accept them as respectable materials in their own right.

Plaster

Plaster is used to provide a smooth, uniform finish over what may be an irregular structural backing. For this purpose a workable mix is needed, though also one that will set to a hard even surface, that will resist cracking and have a uniform texture.

Plasters generally include a binder, a workability agent, aggregate and water.

Binders may be lime (described above, under 'Bricks and brickwork'), though pure lime plasters are soft and little used nowadays, cement (see under 'Bricks and brickwork'), or gypsum. Gypsum is a modified calcium sulphate which occurs naturally, and is also a by-product of the treatment of phosphates with sulphuric acid to produce fertilisers. A hemihydrate gypsum plaster such as plaster of paris sets very rapidly, producing heat, and though useful for casting needs the addition of a retarder such as keratin in normal use. Anhydrous gypsum plaster, such as Keene's, on the other hand, needs the addition of an accelerator, though it sets to a dense, hard body which resists mechanical damage and is useful for arrises.

Non-hydraulic (fat) lime is frequently added to cement and gypsum plasters as a workability agent, though it reduces strength. Air-entraining organic plasticisers are also available.

The aggregate in most plasters is sand (see under 'Bricks and brickwork') though hair was used for this purpose traditionally, improving resistance to cracking, and perlite and exfoliated vermiculite are also used for their peculiar properties. Chapter 3 discusses the selection of plasters for particular circumstances.

Defects

Defects in plaster are more often due to dampness, irregularity or movement in the backing than to the plaster itself. They include:
(a) Bonding failure, often due to damp.
(b) Efflorescence from the masonry forcing the plaster off the wall or deposited on the surface.
(c) Grinning, caused by uneven suction in the backing material.
(d) Popping or blowing, caused by late expansion of insufficiently burnt lime after the initial set.
(e) Crazing, due to overworking.

In Chapter 3 there is a discussion of the advantages and disadvantages of omitting plaster from buildings.

Paint

The purpose of painting is to form an even, flexible coating to protect a surface, usually against the action of damp. Change of colour may be an important objective. The coating must be compatible with the material of the backing, and, if it is to be used externally, weather-resistant.

Paints include binders, such as oil, which dries by a chemical reaction, water, which on drying may induce oxidation of the pigmens, or polymers or copolymers, which dry by evaporation, leaving a resin bonder. In each case, pigment is added for opacity and colour. Many modern pigments are synthetic, and the range of hue and especially chroma is constantly being extended. In addition, there may be a thinner to improve the flow of the material.

Adequate preparation of the surface is vital to success. The paint system normally includes a primer, chosen for compatibility with the background material – for example, etch primer for aluminium, calcium plumbate primer on ferrous metals or lead primer on woodwork—one or two undercoats whose main purpose is to obscure, and a top coat which provides the final colour and finish. The application of paint by roller, brush or spray is largely a matter of convenience. Spraying can only be done over large areas and where careful masking has been carried out, rollers cannot cope with fine detail, and brush application is slow and more difficult to get even.

There are many special-purpose paints for use in particular circumstances, and a manufacturer's advice should be sought if paint has to be applied to an unusual surface, under difficult conditions or where the finished system has to withstand onerous use.

Defects

Defects in paint systems are frequently due to inadequate preparation of the surface. They may include the following:

Bittiness	Due to dirt on the surface under the paint, on the brush or in the paint.
Bleeding	This is caused by the solution of some constituent of the backing material by the paint medium. The surface has been inadequately sealed before painting.
Blistering	Caused by damp trapped behind the paint film, the surface having been wet when painted.
Chalking	This is generally caused by the use of an unsuitable paint in a very exposed situation.
Cracking	This is often due to successive coats having been applied before the previous coat was thoroughly dry, though externally it can be due to age.
Efflorescence	Efflorescence may appear either as a lumpy deposit trapped behind a paint film, or as white salty incrustations on the surface. In the latter case it can be brushed off and will eventually stop, but in the former removal of the paint system and redecoration with a porous material until the washing out of salts ceases is essential.
Flashing	The result of over-rapid setting.
Flaking	Caused by salt or grease on the surface when painted, weak paint film or damp.
Grinning	The backing material shows through, indicating inadequate cover, often due to over-dilution of the paint material.
Pitting	Caused by excessive brushing out, or trapped air, or damp.
Saponification	Alkalis present have converted the oil in the paint into soap.
Sleepiness	Loss of gloss, due to painting in damp conditions.
Wrinkling	Paint applied too thickly.

Character

Paint gives an even and colourful surface to virtually any material, but one which is only temporary and which may obscure the naturally attractive appearance of the structure. Paint should, it is often said, be used only where either its protective qualities or a colour which cannot otherwise be obtained is indispensable. Permanent, natural finishes, especially integral ones, are not only lower in their demands on maintenance but frequently preferred for their appearance. The colour of a painted surface can, however, be easily altered.

Tiles

Clay roofing-tiles

These tiles are manufactured from baked clay in much the same manner as pressed bricks, and may have similar applied textured finishes. They do not need to be entirely non-porous, but have to be highly weather resistant. Too hard a tile is liable to damage by frost.

Concrete tiles

These are less durable in colour but have good weather-resistant properties.

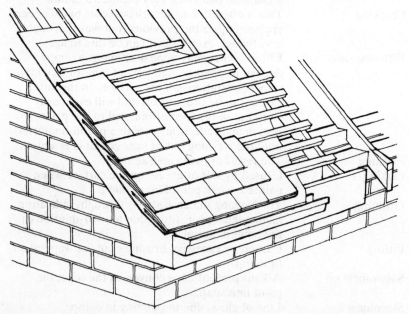

Fig. 2.5 Watertightness of a plain tiled roof demands considerable overlap

The type of tile selected has to be closely related to the pitch. Plain tiles have to be lapped by more than half their length for reasonable weather-tightness, and are therefore heavy. The absence of positive lateral joints makes it necessary for them to be used on steeper pitches, around 45°. (See Fig. 2.5.)

Interlocking tiles save weight because they have positive longitudinal joints and therefore need only a small lap, and they can be used over much shallower pitches, down to 30°. Certain proprietary tiles may be advocated for shallower pitches than those stated, but the manufacturer's advice, in the light of the conditions of exposure, should be obtained before such applications. (See Fig. 2.6.)

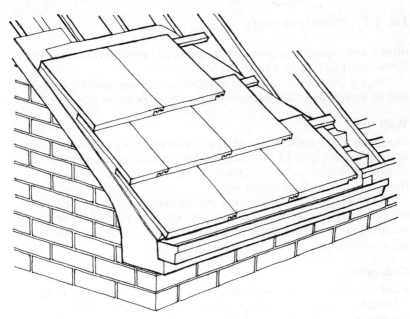

Fig. 2.6 Interlocking tiles can be laid to lower pitches and demand less lap

Tile-hanging

Excellent weatherproofing can be obtained by vertical tile-hanging, though there are sometimes complaints of rattling of the tiles in wind. (See Fig. 2.7.)

Floor tiles

The traditional 'quarry' (or square, from the French 'carré') tile of burnt clay, provides a durable and attractive finish which has good resistance to chemical attack. Unfortunately, these tiles need proper regular maintenance which is not always available. Glazed floor-tiles

Fig. 2.7 Vertical tile-hanging

offer a wide range of colours and patterns and need only to be washed. Either must be laid on a rigid screed.

Plastic tiles can be laid over hardboard on joists, and are lighter, and so they have gained in popularity at the expense of clay tiles.

Wall tiles

Most wall tiles consist of a baked biscuit to which a glaze is fused by firing. They are easy to maintain and have permanence and high resistance to damage to recommend them, and they can be had in frostproof quality for exterior use.

Mosaic, terrazzo, faience and marble may similarly be used as interior or exterior finishes, and are also durable, permanent and easily maintained. A high standard of workmanship is essential to the appearance of all of these materials.

Character

Roof tiles have a traditional irregularity that is supposed to give an informal character to buildings. Modern tiles, however, and particularly interlocking ones, are crisp and regular and lack this softness. The material remains at home with brickwork, since both materials are basically burnt clay.

It is sometimes thought unfortunate that interlocking tiles have come into such nearly universal use for domestic buildings, because of their lightness and suitability to low-pitched roofs. The overall texture of plain tiles is richer, and pantiles or roman tiles have their own rugged character.

The effect of tile-hanging is domestic and yet crisp, and this has been used effectively with prefabricated buildings.

The colours of clay tiles can vary widely, but the 'natural' earth colours of buff, red and brown are generally preferred. It is important that they should be chosen to harmonise with the brickwork. It is the exception for a tiled roof to sit easily over stone masonry.

Quarry tiles have a warm appearance and are less austere than glazed ones. Internal wall-tiling can be cold and lacking in character. Care is needed both in the selection of suitable colours and patterns and in the neat setting out of the joints.

Chapter 3

Selection and use of materials

Clients very often have strong ideas as to the materials they hope to see used in their buildings. These are frequently based on their past experience, and so on out-of-date data, and it is generally much to be preferred that they should be invited to consider a wider range of possibilities on an objective basis.

Parameters

It is usually possible from quite an early stage in the development of a design to establish what the practical and aesthetic parameters of such choices are – and a rational selection of the most suitable available materials should, of course, precede any decision on the form of construction to be adopted.

The client may say that what he requires is a warm surface, or easy maintenance, or durability. The designer must translate such terms into the known characteristics of materials. The most important of these are discussed below.

Strength (See Fig. 3.1.)

The ability to carry mechanical loads without failure. The pressure is called 'Stress' and may be applied as compression, tension, torsion or shear. Characteristically, materials have differing ability to withstand stress, depending on the mode in which it is applied. For most building

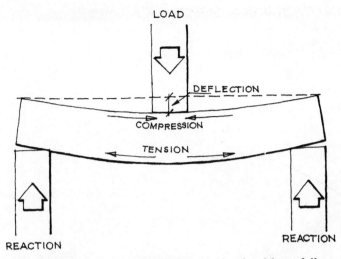

Fig. 3.1 Strength – the ability to carry loads without failure

purposes, the greatest significance attaches to the ability to carry tensile and compressive stresses.

Strength is clearly a vital characteristic of many components of buildings, and detailed calculations will usually be required to establish the optimum sizes of members. What material can suitably be selected, however, can be determined on more general grounds. Note that a factor of safety is generally applied.

Material	Ultimate tensile stress (MN/m^2)	Ultimate compressive stress (MN/m^2)
Engineering bricks class A	—	69.0 –80.00
Engineering bricks class B	—	48.5 –55.00
Concrete	—	10.0 –50.00
Structural timber (softwood)	—	3.00– 9.50 parallel to grain
Sandstone	—	255–195
Limestone	—	15– 42.5
Granite	—	100–330
Mildsteel	400–500	—
Aluminium alloy	300–500	—
Copper	210–350	—
Lead	15	—
Plastics	0.15–0.70	—

Rigidity

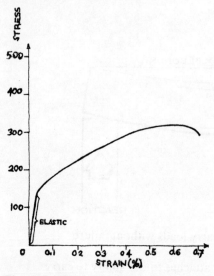

Fig. 3.2 Within the elastic limit, stress varies with strain

Rigidity is measured as the relationship $\dfrac{\text{stress}}{\text{strain}}$, which is known as Young's modulus, or the modulus of elasticity, and shown as 'E'. E is a linear function within the elastic limit of the material: that is to say within the limits of stress during which no permanent deformation (Strain) occurs. The extent to which a beam may deflect or a tie elongate under stress may be of considerable significance to the integrity of the structure as a whole. Damage to finishes is to be expected where excessive strain occurs.

Material	Young's modulus E in GN/m²
Concrete	20
Structural timber	0.5–10
Mild steel	210
Aluminium alloy	70
Copper	100
Lead	14
Plastics	0.2–10

Ductility

In a ductile material, deformation occurs before tensile failure, and the material is therefore 'workable'. Ductility is measured by 'percentage

elongation' in a standard test. Particularly ductile materials include
lead, copper and some plastics.

Toughness

A material of good strength and ductility is considered tough, and will
withstand shock loads. Copper is tough.

Brittleness

Brittleness is the reverse of toughness. Brittle materials break without
deformation, and are stronger in compression than in tension. Cast
iron is comparatively brittle.

Hardness

The Brinell hardness test measures the indentation caused by a steel
ball dropped on to a material under standard conditions. A Brinell
number, based on the results of this test, gives a guide to the relative
hardness of the material. The higher the number, the better the
material will resist abrasion, and so the more durable against wear it
will be. Figure 3.3 shows a test rig.

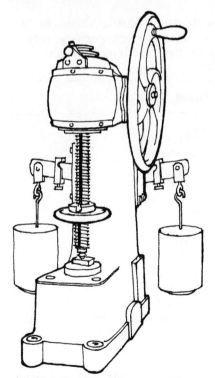

Fig. 3.3 Brinell test for hardness

Material	Brinell no.
Steel	120–150
Aluminium alloy	60–100
Copper	40–100
Lead	4

Resilience

Resilience is the energy stored by a material – the extent to which it will recover quickly from strain. It is a significant factor in comfort, for example, in floors. Resilient floor-coverings such as rubber are found less tiring to those using them than harder materials would be.

Density

Density is the mass of unit volume of a material, for building purposes generally expressed in kg/m^3. This figure should be distinguished from specific gravity.

Relative density

The ratio of the density of a material to that of a similar volume of water at 4°C. Relatively 'heavy' materials have a high specific gravity. Weight is the pull of gravity acting on a mass, and is measured in newtons.

Material	Density in kg/m^3
Brickwork	1 250–2 250
Concrete	2 250–2 500
Structural timber	400–600
Sandstone	2 000–2 750
Limestone	2 000–2 400
Granite	2 500–3 200
Mild steel	7 800
Aluminium	2 700
Copper	9 000
Lead	11 250
Plastics	900–2 500

Since the loads imposed by each material in the building have to be transmitted to, and eventually carried by, the foundations, important savings can be made by choosing materials of low density.

Thermal conductivity (k) (See Fig. 3.4.)

Thermal conductivity is the reciprocal of the resistivity, and varies with

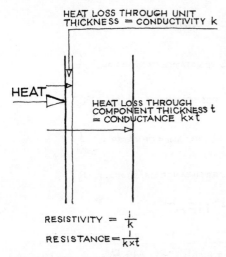

Fig. 3.4 Resistivity is the reciprocal of conductivity

the density of the material. It measures the rate of heat transfer between the faces of a material, and is stated in W/mK

Conductivity × thickness gives the conductance through an actual component.

Material	k in W/m K
Brickwork	1.50–0.75
Concrete	1.5
Lightweight concrete	0.35–0.60
Structural timber	0.150
Chipboard	0.100–0.160
Wood wool	0.01
Limestone	1.5
Steel	60
Plaster	0.50
Fibreglass quilt	0.03–0.04

Thermal transmittance (U) (See Fig. 3.5.)

Thermal transmittance measures the rate of heat transfer from air to air through what may be a complex structure. It is stated in W/m² K and is the reciprocal of the sum of the resistances including those of cavities and surfaces. It is significant in heat-loss calculations, which (however) need to take into account also convected losses and the degree of exposure and emissivity of surfaces.

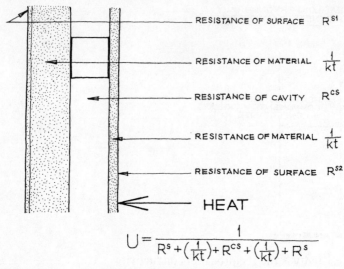

RESISTANCE OF SURFACE R^{s1}

RESISTANCE OF MATERIAL $\frac{1}{kt}$

RESISTANCE OF CAVITY R^{cs}

RESISTANCE OF MATERIAL $\frac{1}{kt}$

RESISTANCE OF SURFACE R^{s2}

HEAT

$$U = \frac{1}{R^s + \left(\frac{1}{kt}\right) + R^{cs} + \left(\frac{1}{kt}\right) + R^s}$$

Fig. 3.5 U value indicates heat lost through the whole construction

Assembly	U in W/m² K
Plain tiles on battens, plasterboard ceiling, 25 mm fibreglass quilt	0.91
50 mm wood wool deck, felt finish	1.24
Cavity wall, insulation block inner leaf, plaster one face	0.97–1.31
Double glazing, 6 mm air space	3.00

Thermal expansion coefficient

Thermal expansion is often important to the design of buildings, and

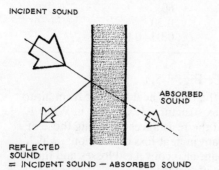

INCIDENT SOUND

ABSORBED SOUND

REFLECTED SOUND = INCIDENT SOUND − ABSORBED SOUND

Fig. 3.6 Absorption coefficient indicates the amount of sound not reflected

should be predicted as accurately as possible, in order that suitable expansion joints can be designed and incorporated into the structure. Thermal movement is responsible for much damage to buildings. (See Ch. 10.)

The movement to be anticipated is expressed by the coefficient of thermal expansion, which shows the increase in length per unit length for each rise of 1 °C in temperature.

Material	Coefficient of thermal expansion $\times 10^{-6}$
Brickwork	5–7
Concrete	10–14
Limestone	3–10
Sandstone	7–16
Granite	8–10
Mild steel	12
Aluminium alloy	24
Copper	17
Lead	30

If a material is prevented from moving with temperature changes, internal and potentially damaging stresses are set up.

Sound absorption (See Fig. 3.6.)

The absorption coefficient shows the proportion of sound of a particular frequency falling upon a surface which will fail to be reflected from it. The absorption is in some cases due to dissipation of the energy within the structure of the material and in other cases to it being allowed to pass right through. Frequency affects the 'pitch' of a sound, and is measured in hertz (Hz) or cycles per second.

Sound absorption is of great importance in establishing suitable acoustic conditions in spaces.

Material	Absorption coefficient at		
	125 Hz	500 Hz	2 000 Hz
Plaster	0.02	0.02	0.04
Insulating board	0.3	0.3	0.3
Brickwork	0.02	0.02	0.04
Panelling	0.4	0.15	0.1
Glass	0.2	0.1	0.05
Open window	100	100	100
Audience, per person	0.17	0.43	0.47

Sound insulation

Absorbent surfaces will improve the quality of sound within a room, but will have little effect on the sound passing through a structure. This is measured in decibels (dB) and improvement can generally only be made by either (a) increasing the weight of the structure or (b) divorcing the structure from that to which the sound would otherwise be transmitted.

Assembly	Sound reduction in decibels at 500 Hz (air-borne)
Half-brick wall, plastered two sides	45
Cavity wall, plastered one face	55
Window (closed)	24
Double windows, space not less than 200 mm	40

Reflectance

Reflectance is a measure of the percentage of incident light which is reflected from a surface. The 'value' of a colour in the Munsell system is related to reflectance, V ($V-1$) giving the approximate light reflectance of the surface. If the surface is rough in texture, however, extra energy will be absorbed into it, and if it is glossy the proportion of reflected light will be increased, so that this approximate measure applies only to matt or eggshell finishes.

Vapour resistance

Vapour resistance, which is the inverse of permeability, may be stated in MN s/g for unit thickness. It is of considerable significance to the choice of DPCs and vapour barriers.

Material		Vapour resistance MN s/g
Brickwork	100 mm	2.5–10.00
Concrete	100 mm	3.0–10.00
Timber	50 mm	2.0–4.0
Rendering	12 mm	1.0–1.5
Gloss paint system		7.5–40
Polythene	0.06 mm	250
Aluminium foil		4 000

Electrical resistance

The resistance of a structure through which a current passes is defined as the ratio $\dfrac{\text{voltage drop}}{\text{current (amps)}}$. Resistance is the reciprocal of the rate at which current will flow through the material. An insulating material has a high resistance, while a conductor has a low one. The sum of the resistance in a circuit must equal the total power being used. Resistance is measured in ohms (Ω).

The conductivities of metals are stated as percentages of that of copper under standard conditions.

Material	% conductivity (= 1/ resistivity)
Mild steel	12
Aluminium alloy	32–52
Copper	100
Lead	8

Behaviour in fire

Combustibility

The flashpoint of a substance is the temperature at which it gives off a

Material	Behaviour in fire			
	Flame spread	Toxic vapours	Combustion	Loss of strength
Brickwork	Nil	No	No	Loss of supporting structures
Concrete	Nil	No	No	Cracking due to expansion of reinforcement
Structural timber	Low	Yes	Yes	Some
Steel	Nil	No	No	Yes, above 400 °C
Aluminium	Nil	No	No	Yes, above 200 °C
Plastics	Medium to rapid	Yes	Yes	Yes
Wood wool slabs	very low	Yes	Yes	Yes, if saturated by fire hoses
Glass	Nil	No	No	Shatters

flammable vapour–that is, one which can be ignited. Heat is required as well as oxygen and the fuel (the vapour) for materials with a flashpoint above normal temperatures to maintain combustion.

Besides producing gases which are toxic, many materials undergo considerable loss of strength in fire.

Flame spread

The maintenance and spread of flame as well as loss of strength need to be considered in selecting materials for situations where there is either a fire hazard or potential difficulty in evacuating the building in emergency. Materials in which the products of combustion obstruct the passage of oxygen are likely to be self-extinguishing.

Clay products in general, having already been fired to high temperatures, withstand fire well, but they may become unstable due to the loss of support from adjacent structures, such as timber beams. Timbers maintain and moderately spread flame, though surface charring may protect the unburnt core of the member and retain some residual strength. Steel loses strength severely at temperatures above 400 °C though it is itself incombustible.

Other characteristics

Less quantifiable, but still eminently desirable characteristics may include ease of cleaning, appearance, and associative qualities (for example, marble associated with formality, stained softwood with more relaxed situations).

Cost is important in almost every case. Not only will a cost ceiling be thrown-up by the cost plan, but consideration of terotechnological factors should lead to attention being paid to costs of maintenance and replacement.

Deterioration

The life of every material used in building is limited, though many forms of protection are available to lengthen their life. Causes of decay include:
(a) *Metal corrosion* (see Ch. 2).
(b) *Damage by water and frost* (See Ch. 11).
(c) *Biological attack on timber* (See Ch. 12).
(d) *Atmospheric pollution* (See Ch. 13).
(e) *Abrasion*. In hospitals and industrial premises, surfaces may have to withstand constant hard wear, and this may be the most important factor in the selection of the material.
(f) *Attack by chemicals*. Especially soluble sulphates in ground water attacking cement.
(g) *Faulty maintenance*. Occupants should be provided with a guide to the correct maintenance of their property, to avoid damage by over enthusiastic cleaning or the misapplication of cleaning materials.

(h) *Sunlight*. Loss of paint colour and the degradation of some varnishes can result from exposure to ultra-violet radiation.

(i) *Crystallisation of soluble salts*. May have an adverse effect on natural stones and under-fired clay products.

Design specification

As was briefly indicated above, it is almost always advantageous to prepare a design specification based on considerations of the kind discussed as an aid to the selection of materials. Instead of following existing practice which may have become outdated by new developments, and choosing from a limited range of familiar options, the analysis involved in preparing such a document is likely to result in fresh thinking. Armed with the definitions of the levels of thermal transmittance, reflectance, hardness, resilience, toughness and so on required the designer can investigate the whole range of materials available, making appropriate tests where necessary.

In some cases the development of a new product may be essential if the criteria are to be met in full, and this is not an unconceivable strategy. The plastics industry, in particular, has responded throughout its life to new requirements for new applications.

To take a simple example, in the case of a proposed home for old people, the management might wish the floor finish for toilets to be water-resistant, resilient, easily cleaned, light in colour and durable. The cost target would be known.

Water resistance is associated with permeability, but also with the jointing techniques adopted. If the floor is to be truly resistant to water it is probably best to select a jointless material, though the use of one with watertight joints should not be excluded. In order to determine the resilience of a material it may be necessary to compare its performance with familar ones under standard conditions. It should be possible to state, for example, that the resilience should be at least equal to that of 5 mm rubber. Ease of cleaning immediately excludes any material which needs to be polished for its own protection, such as wood block. Light colour is associated with high value, so that it can be stated that a value of 6 or above is acceptable (reflectance $6 \times 5 = 30$ per cent). Durability is related to both toughness and hardness. Ductility could be essential if there is likely to be any structural movement, since cracking would result in loss of the necessary waterproof qualities.

Much of the selection process will, of course, be relative. It is only in very stringent circumstances that precise degrees of, say, acid resistance or strength might be mandatory in a finish. None the less, consideration of the desirable qualities in an analytical way has much to recommend it.

Where a component of the fabric is under consideration, more exact quantification would be necessary.

If a sandwich construction were being designed for the infill panels between windows in an external envelope, very precise levels of thermal transmittance, sound absorption and rigidity could be determined. The design specification for such a component might include such statements as that:

(a) Total thermal transmittance not to exceed 1.00 W/m^{2}K.
(b) Young's modulus not to be less than 10 GN/m^2.
(c) Vapour resistivity not to be less than 150 MN s/g m.
(d) Reduction in transmission of sound not to be less than 50 dB.
(e) External surface to require no maintenance.
(f) Thickness not to exceed 150 mm.

On such a basis it is possible to develop a panel which will fulfil the essential criteria in as simple a manner as possible, by study of the known characteristics of materials.

Certain materials where selection from a range of possibilities is necessary are now considered.

Bricks

The characteristics most likely to concern designers where bricks are concerned are strength, porosity, durability and appearance.

Strength

Bricks are generally considered to be capable of carrying only compressive loads, though work on the ability of brickwork to withstand tension is being carried out.

It is important to consider not only the compressive strength of the bricks but also that of the mortar (which should be selected to match the strength of the bricks) and that of the whole masonry.

Porosity

The porosity of bricks is quoted as a percentage by weight of water taken up during standard tests. Bricks for use in DPCs should absorb no more than 4.5 per cent. Most bricks have porosity well in excess of this figure, with obvious dangers if freezing occurs when they are saturated. The only advisable method of avoiding bricks which would be damaged in such circumstances is to choose ones which can be shown to have survived in practice.

Durability

Bricks of burnt clay are in general very durable. Decay may result from attack by water containing calcium sulphates washing-off limestone, and sulphates may also attack mortar.

Appearance

Facing-bricks should usually be selected on the basis of trial panels

Backing	Adhesion	Mix		Finish
Brickwork	Good	1 cement : 2 lime : 8 sand		Roughcast
Concrete	Low (use bonder)	1 cement : 1 lime : 5 sand		Float
Lath	Good	1 : 3 cement/sand		Scraped

The choice of an open texture and minimum cement content is generally recommended, for resistance to mechanical damage.

which have been exposed for a whole season rather than from individual samples. The overall appearance is affected by the amount of variation of colour between bricks, and by the colour of the mortar.

A homogeneous appearance is most often preferred, and this should be judged in conditions as close as possible to those from which the brickwork will eventually be viewed.

Timber

Strength, length of members available, figure, colour and hardness are all significant in the selection of timber.

The classification under each of these headings of most available timbers is widely available, though since the quality of any natural material is likely to vary it may well be desirable to subject samples to testing if performance in any respect is critical.

The most durable species are the dense hardwoods, such as teak – which may last unprotected for more than twenty-five years – but few softwoods could be expected to last for more than ten years in similar conditions. In practice, all timber should be maintained in dry conditions, and either pressure impregnated with preservative or painted or varnished.

Apart from the selection of major loadbearing members on the ground of strength, the most usual criteria for the selection of a wood will be regularity and appearance, for joinery. Stained and varnished samples should be inspected, where figure is important, and if a bold figure is anticipated the samples should approximate to the size of the completed element. A vigorous figure which appears attractive in a small sample can be overwhelming when used in the panelling of an entire room.

Stone

It is unlikely that any natural stone which might be chosen for use in this country would prove to be inadequate in compressive strength. Durability, too, is high.

The choice is more likely to be made on grounds of appearance, and the appearance of the completed masonry will be affected by three major factors:
(a) The natural colour and texture of the selected stone.
(b) The type of masonry, from random rubble to coursed ashlar, which is chosen. (See Fig. 3.7.)
(c) The working of the face of the stones. (See Fig. 3.8.)

The wide variety available in each of these respects makes this a delicate and influential area of design. It is often best to follow two rules:

Fig. 3.7 Masonry types

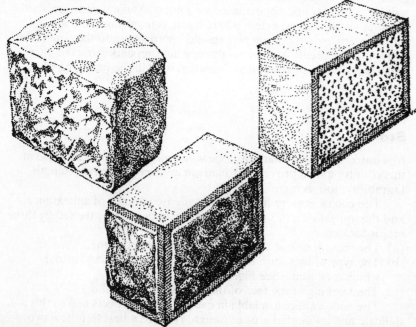

Fig. 3.8 Surface-working of stone

1. Use the locally occurring stone if it is at all possible, especially if there is much stonework in existing buildings.
2. Allow the degree of formality of the masonry chosen to reflect the character of the building, so that while coursed rubble may be used for a country house, ashlar would be a better choice for a city-centre building.

Stone is, of course, frequently used in claddings to framed and brick structures. It is generally preferred that the pattern of jointing in such cases should not ape that of structural masonry.

Plaster

No plaster coat should be stronger than the backing to which it is applied, and a balance needs to be struck between durability and density. Arrises in softer plasterwork should be protected by beads or worked in Keene's cement.

Backing	Preparation	Material	Thickness (mm)
Brickwork or insulation block	Good natural key	1 : 2 : 3 lime gypsum sand or Class B gypsum plaster	12
Concrete	Remove oil with detergent. Bonder	Thin wall gypsum plaster, sprayed	10
Plasterboard	Scrim joints	Thin wall gypsum plaster	5
Expanded metal lathing		1 : 2 Class B sand with hairs	10–13

Renderings

Renderings should normally be used for appearance rather than as a method of waterproofing.

Chapter 4

Detailing

Introduction

Detailing is an integral part of the design process, and should not be thought of as a discrete stage in the evolution of a project. The same principles apply as to any other aspect of the development.

It is necessary to examine the particular problem, and to determine precisely what constraints govern the solution. This must be done from the following three points of view.

1. *Function*. What practical requirements is the detail intended to fulfil? Are there limitations on size or weight?
2. *Aethetics*. The appearance of the detail may very well have a significant effect on the appearance of the entire building, and this must be borne in mind throughout the development of the detail. If delicacy, or a robust effect, a particular proportion or a chosen texture or colour is vital to the aesthetic this may be a major consideration during design.
3. *Technology*. The detailer must apply a sound knowledge of what is technically feasible. He must not only grasp the range of available materials and know the capabilities of each, but also understand the ways in which each can be worked and jointed effectively and economically. He also needs to be aware of the order in which components will be assembled, and of the need to simplify the erection process wherever this can be done without disadvantage.

Once this analysis has been carried out, it is essential to determine the priorities within the established constraints. An overriding

52

condition will always be that the results of earlier decision-making processes must be accepted: it is basic to the smooth functioning of the entire decision-making and design process that the most influential decisions are made first and then regarded as final. It must be clearly understood where compromises can and cannot be made.

The detailer proceeds to develop more than one possible solution to the problem before him, trying to avoid the automatic adoption of well-tried solutions (though of course these will sometimes prove appropriate.)

Eventually it becomes clear that a particular potential detail is likely to be the most fruitful to follow through. The detail can then be finalised.

As well as being satisfactory in itself, the detail must be properly related to every other feature of the design. This is easiest to achieve if a horizontal and a vertical datum are established, to which all features are related. In its most developed – and useful – form this evolves into a three-dimensional grid which as well as locating features and space in relation to each other is a considerable aid to both design and site setting-out. (See Fig. 4.1.) When this principle is adopted the set of drawings for the job can be greatly simplified.

It is far easier to develop a satisfying and coherent overall design if at any rate the major features are detailed at a very early stage in the process – at the stage, indeed, of the assimilation of data on which the design is based. They then become part of the technical vocabulary

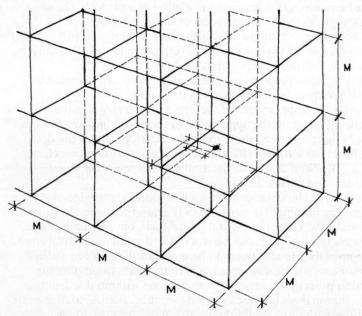

Fig. 4.1 The planning grid gives unity as well as aiding design

adopted for the job. In the days of a widely accepted vernacular of constructional methods – or indeed of 'pattern books' – this was the implicit, if not always recognised, practice. An elevation could be drawn without first drafting details of eaves or window openings because the way in which these features would be put together was well understood. This is not the case today. Few buildings have 'textbook' details, and there is continual evolution. It would be irresponsible of an Architect to show his client sketches of a neat, unfussy, façade without first having satisfied himself that such an appearance could be achieved without detriment to the practical sides of the job. He must feel assured that practical details which will achieve that effect can be devised. He must equally be willing to accept a less conventional appearance if a thoroughly practical detail throws one up – or at least to be sufficiently open-minded to consider the possibility.

Details should not in the first instance be drawn in the form of simple sections. It is essential that the full three-dimensional implications of decisions should be understood. For example, it is at the junction of the vertical and horizontal components of a window frame, and of the opening in masonry it may fill, that complications are likely to arise. (See Fig. 4.2.)

Sectional drawings may well be the most effective way of conveying the designer's intentions to the builder, though this is not

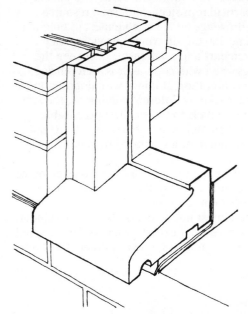

Fig. 4.2 It is essential for the detailer to consider his proposals three-dimensionally

necessarily the case: if the detail is in any way an unconventional one they can be a most dangerous development tool. The detailer needs to cultivate the ability to sketch his intentions in simple perspective form, so that he can satisfy himself that the detail 'works'.

The information needed by the Quantity Surveyor and, later, the builder, is different. They should be confident that the detail is practicable and the component fulfils the requirements. They need to know what materials are to be used, what labours are required and how and where the part is to be assembled. The eventual detail drawings and schedules, which will usually be related to simplified layout drawings and a grid such as that described above, should contain no information beyond that required for these purposes: anything more is liable to result in confusion, and even conflict between one drawing and another. It should always be the aim to simplify the set of production drawings eventually issued to the point where they contain NO redundant information and NO repetition.

This implies that two sets of details will be prepared – the one made during development, which proves that the details work, and the other for use during construction.

It is common for a team to work together on the development of the details for a job: they must be prepared to consult one another regularly and to accept the effects of team decisions on each member's work. They must establish an acceptable order of working by which the most influential decisions will be the earliest to be taken.

Details developed for a particular project can form a resource book – indeed, to make such drawings on A4-sized paper, to bind in a folder, is simple and convenient. Layout drawings, providing they acknowledge the space requirements and relationships between the details can be outline drawings only, with copious cross-referencing.

There is little virtue in a proliferation of minor variations among a set of details. Unless there are markedly different conditions, the aim should be to limit the number of details to the smallest practicable amount. Repetition is not only economic sense, but also aids the unity of the overall design. Details throughout a scheme should be compatible and evidently logical.

The practice of building-up a bank of 'standard' details in an office has some advantages, provided only tested details are added to the bank, and the store is rigorously kept up-to-date. Where this is done, the task of analysis in every case must not be overlooked. The standard detail must not be used simply because it exists: it can only be adopted where it can clearly be shown to meet the precise requirements of the case.

Influences upon details

The problem to be solved by any particular detail is likely to have a number of aspects. Some of these are referred to below.

Weather

All buildings must withstand the effects of the weather, which may be extreme, and yet few of the materials used in buildings are actually weatherproof. These have to be used so as to minimise the worst effects of the climate, which include the following.

Rain including driving rain

The annual rainfall is a poor indicator of the intensity of rainfall which may occur, and it is preferable to consult tables showing the likely incidence of particular intensities of rain in the location involved. Gutters are often designed to remove precipitation at a rate of 75 mm per hour overall: tables indicate the frequency with which such a rate of rainfall may be expected to be exceeded, and suitable arrangements must be made to deal with any excess without causing an unacceptable hazard such as the overflow of foul sewers.

The BRE Index of driving rain is helpful both in determining the likely penetration of rain into masonry and the amount of run-off from pitched roofs and vertical faces during conditions of combined rain and wind.

Wind

In addition to the loads which the wind can impose upon a structure, the designer should be aware that movements of wind between buildings can result in perhaps unanticipated pressure and suction. The turbulence created between high blocks can result in virtually permanent winds in such areas, spoiling an otherwise pleasant

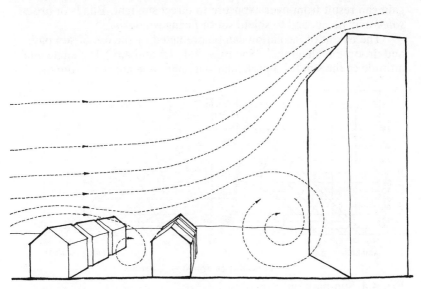

Fig. 4.3 Turbulance has to be considered

environment. Conditions in which it is practically impossible to keep external doors closed, because of this action, are known. (See Fig. 4.4.) The effect can to some extent be relieved by allowing gaps through the bases of the buildings, though the wind speed at such points will still be high.

Modern lightweight construction may mean that roof decks (for example) cannot be relied on to stay in position through their own weight, but need to be physically tied down. Where there is turbulence around the building, the tendency of the roof to rise may be exacerbated.

Snow

The depth of snow will be considerably more than that of similar precipitation in the form of rain, and must be allowed for in deciding the depths of flashings. Snow often slips from pitched roofs as minor avalanches at the onset of thaw, and can crash through glass roofs below. These should be protected by snowboards along the upper gutter.

Mist and fog

Penetration of fog into a building can lead to increased levels of condensation. (See Ch. 11.)

Sun

It is usually considered desirable that any habitable room should receive the sun for at least part of every day. The obverse of this coin is that both glare and unacceptable levels of temperature due to solar gain can result from over exposure to direct sunlight. Blinds or *brises soleil* may be needed to shield south-facing windows.

The extent of insolation can be predicted by the use of sun path and droop-line diagrams. (See Figs. 4.4, 4.5 and 4.6.) The angle and altitude of the sun for a particular date and time are read from the

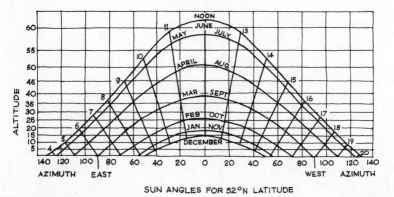

SUN ANGLES FOR 52°N LATITUDE

Fig. 4.4 Sun-path diagram

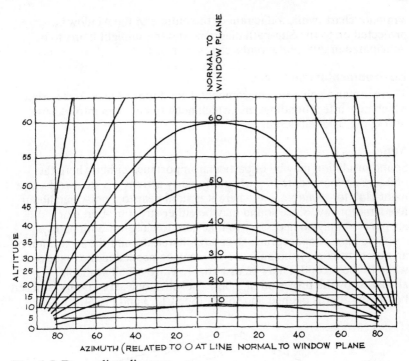

Fig. 4.5 Droop-line diagram

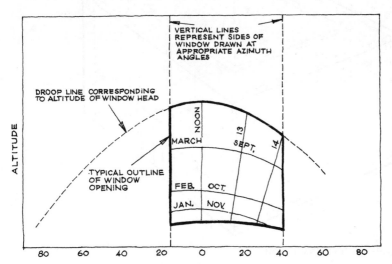

Fig. 4.6 The prediction of insolation

58

sun-path chart, while a diagram of the outline of the window is
projected on to the Sun-path diagram, and the sunlight hours to be
anticipated in different months can be read off.

Environmental conditions

There are also common environmental conditons of man-made origin
which may affect buildings and which need to be taken into account
during the detailed design.

Noise

Sound insulation may be of particular importance either where the
building accommodates a particularly noisy activity – a steelworks or a
night-club for example – or where it is sited near to a noisy neighbour,
like a motorway. Since sound may be either structure-borne or
air-borne it may be necessary to take care to close-off both paths.

Selection of appropriate structural materials, and the separation of
an outer structure from an inner one may be needed in the first case,
while in the second it may be essential to close-off all available
air-paths, by the provision of lobbies in which one set of doors is closed
before another is opened and so on. (See Ch. 3 and Fig. 4.7.)

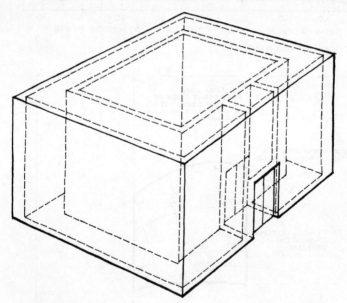

Fig. 4.7 Sound insulation

Vibration

Where continual vibration is anticipated – for example, where a
building is sited close to a motorway – it is usually advisable to detail

every part of the building so that small movements can be absorbed before damage is caused. In effect, the choice of gaskets rather than hard jointings, and care that glazing is not so tightly fixed that it will crack directly movement occurs, should result in frequent small expansion or movement joints being incorporated in the building.

Pollution

Atmospheric pollution is less important today than it once was, due to the Clean Air Acts. In industrial areas, where damage from air pollution can still be anticipated, however, the advice of the Environmental Health Officer as to the content to be expected should be obtained, and materials and particularly finishes chosen accordingly. In most polluted atmospheres it is wise to avoid the use of limestones or calcareous sandstones, which may be decayed by sulphur dioxide, in favour of other materials, and zinc should not be used. Chlorinated rubber paints have good acid-resistance.

Attack

Buildings may also be subjected to attack, and need to be designed to resist it.

Security

It is a virtually universal requirement that it should be possible to leave a building untenanted without endangering the contents. Attention has to be paid not only to the locks and latches on doors and windows, but also to means of permanent ventilation and to trellises and similar features which may provide convenient ladders for marauders. The advice of the Crime Prevention Officer at the local police headquarters is usually freely available.

In the case of more severe risks – banks, research establishments or prisons, for example – the client is likely to have considerable expertise and to insist that this is applied. It will be necessary not only to design a secure building but also to ensure that details of the means of defence are treated as confidential, so that even within the design and construction team some information is disseminated on a limited basis.

Vandalism

Vandalism is apparently an increasing problem in public places which are not under constant observation, such as public toilets, subways, and the access areas of blocks of flats. Some success has been claimed for a general upgrading of environmental standards in such areas, as people generally are said to respond to their surroundings, and spartan conditions evoke a rough-and-ready response. This is certainly not a universal answer, however, and it is one many Clients would hesitate to apply. Considerable advances are constantly being made in the development of vandalproof light-switches, plumbing and even paints.

It may be preferable to provide finishes which can be readily washed down rather than attempt to choose materials which are not susceptible to graffiti.

Movement

Constant movement due to shifting loads, changes of temperature and changes of moisture content are to be anticipated in all buildings, which should be flexible enough to receive them without damage. In particular, regular thermal expansion joints, which pass through the entire building, should be incorporated in all buildings at intervals not greater than about 30 m, though allowance for movement should be made in all dry joints. (See also Ch. 10, and Fig. 4.8.)

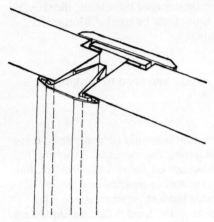

Fig. 4.8 Expansion joint

Fire

Designers need to be acutely aware of the potential dangers of fire, and to bear this firmly in mind from three points of view:

1. The selection of materials which will not maintain combustion. Materials are graded according to both fire resistance and flame spread. (See Ch. 3.)
2. Smoke must be prevented from reaching and blocking escape routes, requiring the use of self-closing doors, and the avoidance of shatterable glass.
3. Escape routes must be planned to give alternative means of egress to the open air, to avoid confusion in the darkness and panic which may accompany the emergency evacuation of a building, and to be adequate for the entire population of the building.

The advice of the Fire Prevention Officer of the local brigade is freely available.

Natural lighting

The need for well-distributed natural lighting is clearly significant to the shape and positioning of windows. Windows on two sides of a space will usually provide more uniform illumination than can be obtained on one side of a room alone, and roof lights are an efficient means of natural lighting. Since illumination levels at working height are critical, cills below that level do not improve lighting. Use of the BRE Sky Component Protractors allows the lighting to be provided to be quantified in advance.

Ventilation

Permanent ventilation may be desirable for many spaces, and ventilator lights which can be controllably opened to provide natural ventilation without large windows having to be opened are almost always necessary. The number of air changes per hour which are required may be specified, and this will control the area of opening lights: it should be noted that the most efficient and controllable natural ventilation is obtained from double-hung vertical sliding sashes on two sides of a space.

Exclusion of water

All details should be critically scrutinised to ensure that they provide

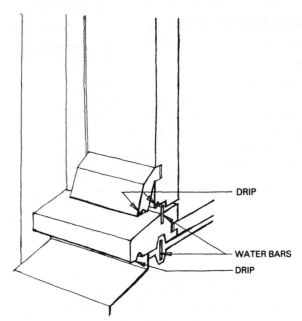

Fig. 4.9 Water must be excluded

adequate defence against the ingress of water. Not only must all DPCs and DPMs be continuous and well lapped, but the following points should be examined.

Falls

Horizontal surfaces should be avoided unless a sufficient depth of water is to be retained to avoid differential thermal movement. Even where a pool of some depth is proposed it is generally convenient to provide a fall to the base so that the water can be efficiently drained when necessary. Water should be collected in a properly drained gutter if it is present in any quantity (the rain from a roof or the exposed vertical face of a multi-storey building, being cases in point).

The drainage of such gutters may be by down-pipes to drains or through gargoyles of which a feature is made, but must be planned to be adequate in all circumstances.

The water from small features such as cills or copings is usually allowed to drip. It is likely to seep back along the lower surface of the feature unless a capillary groove is provided, where the water will collect before dripping harmlessly to the earth. It is often desirable, as well, to incorporate a water-bar as a further positive barrier to the entry of water below the feature. (See Fig. 4.9.)

Particular features requiring care

Attention is particularly directed to the need for care in detailing at the following points.

Joints and junctions (See Ch. 15)

Note that the tolerances required to allow for inaccuracy in manufacture and setting-out, and to provide manoevring space for construction, make the design of joints particularly critical in the case of dry construction. Where metal is to be placed next to masonry, a timber subframe, which can be scribed, is likely to improve the joint.

The junction between old and new work is especially important, since the new construction must be expected to show some movement as it dries-out and settles. Such a junction should, therefore, be designed deliberately to accept movement without damage, and in particular the foundations should be entirely separate.

Roofs and roof coverings

The relationship between roof covering and fall should be carefully conformed with. While in general the smaller the unit of roof covering the steeper the fall this is not universally applicable, and the advice of the manufacturer of the covering should be followed.

The need for ventilation of roof spaces should not be forgotten.

This ventilation can often most conveniently be provided at the eaves soffit.

A new and heavier covering should never be placed on an existing roof structure without careful prior calculation to establish that this can be done without damage.

Cavity walls
Cill, lintol, jamb and eaves details, in particular, need to be scrutinised with care to ensure that the cavity is not bridged and that all necessary DPCs have been included. In particular, a perspective sketch is necessary to ensure that there is no vulnerable joint where horizontal and vertical components of the damp proofing meet. (See Fig. 4.10.)

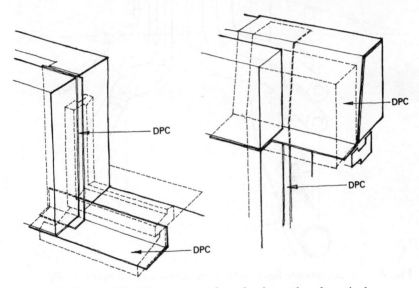

Fig. 4.10 Vulnerable joints occur where horizontal and vertical components meet

Earth under rafts
The earth under raft foundations is liable to erosion by the rain. Care should be taken to provide protection, probably in the form of a paved strip. This should not be wide enough to be used as a path, since people using it would be liable to walk into open windows.

Sheathings and claddings
The edges of thin claddings are especially vulnerable, and need to be protected. Water entering here can lead to the disintegration of the panel.

Ducts

When laying out service ducts it needs to be remembered that junctions and bends have to be accommodated as well as the straight pipes. Access to pipes at the back of ducts without disturbance to other services is also essential. Ducts may, therefore, need to be rather larger than might appear necessary at first glance. This is a case where designing three-dimensionally is essential. (See Fig. 4.11.)

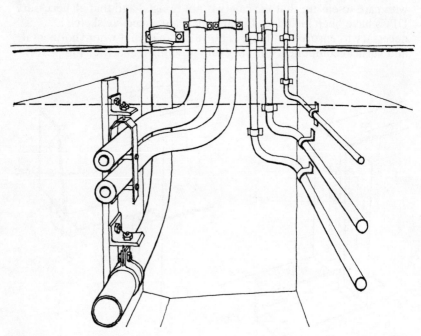

Fig. 4.11 Duct layouts have to be considered three-dimensionally

Cost

Costs may be significantly affected by detailed design, and detailers should keep the following factors firmly in mind.

Standardisation

Standardisation and repetition are relatively cheap, because they make the craftsman's and the manager's work easier. There is little virtue in avoidable variety. This does not mean that the overall design need degenerate into boredom, but that each change should be carefully considered and seen to be necessary.

Price and availability of materials

There are constant fluctuations in the costs of materials, which can be particularly severely affected by unexpected shortages. The Builder's advice is invaluable in this respect, and this is one reason for the often-expressed wish to involve the Builder more closely in the design stages of the project.

Cost of labour

As a percentage of overall costs, the cost of skilled labour is ever increasing.

There is a strong case for simplifying construction, so that the services of the craftsman are reserved for those parts of the construction where he is irreplaceable. One result of this fact is the ever-increasing use of specialised plant: if this is to be used most efficiently, the detailer needs to know its capabilities and limitations. Though he may not limit the work he asks for to the ability of the available plant entirely, his knowledge of what is possible will enable him to use it wherever this is sensible.

Transport and handling

Large components transported for long distances, especially if elaborate handling equipment is needed for loading and unloading, will be disproportionately expensive. The detailer ought to be aware of the capacities of plant, the sizes of lorries, and the expense of importing special cranes, so that he limits the size and weight of imported components as sensibly as possible. He should also appreciate that components are particularly vulnerable to damage during handling, and ensure that such parts are of sufficiently rugged construction.

Chapter 5

The specification

The art of specification-writing is sadly too often neglected by Architects and their assistants. This can have the result either that standard clauses are selected repetitively and without proper thought or that the responsibility for defining what is required falls by default upon the Quantity Surveyor.

Quantity Surveyors have, of course, a wide experience (and vocabulary) of specification clauses, and can usually produce one which seems to them to be about right for the circumstances to provide a basis for competitive tendering. It is a very limited view of the specification that assumes that this is its principal or only function.

The specification is the appropriate document to describe all those aspects of the work which cannot be shown on the drawings. It should be complementary to, and not duplicate, material conveyed by the drawings and schedules. The information required can only be provided by the designer, who alone knows the conditions, materials and quality he envisages. It is for him to convey this prescription clearly and concisely, and this can be done only if it is set against his well-ordered knowledge both of materials and construction generally and of the requirements of the particular job. An essential basis for the preparation of the specification is concentrated thought to determine what standards are required in the light of the standards that can reasonably be achieved. The writer must know why he is making particular demands, and that they are within the bounds of possibility, although this information will not usually be included in the document.

Uses

The specification will be used in three separate but important ways.

1. By the design team as a reference to decisions arrived at. As their proposals are developed, so notes on the material requirements and possibly the conditions under which the work will have to be carried out, including in particular the standards to be accepted and methods of quality control to be adopted will be added to a pool. This must always be done in the light of previous decisions, with which later ones must be compatible. (See Fig. 5.1.)

Fig. 5.1 The specification is a design tool

2. By the Quantity Surveyor, when he is preparing the preamble to the Bill of Quantities, and the detailed descriptions of measured items. He should never be left in doubt as to what is required, and the specification must, for his purposes, indicate particularly any variation from normal practice, so that this can be plainly drawn to the attention of tenderers.

   Where tenders for small jobs are invited on the basis of drawings and specification alone, the specification will of course be directly read by the Estimator, and should give him all that information he needs to prepare his tender, which cannot be obtained from the drawings. (See Fig. 5.2.)

3. As a site reference to the standards envisaged by the designer and tendered for by the Contractor, and a guide to the tests and quality checks required. Neither the Site Agent nor the Clerk of Works will normally have been a party to either the design or tendering

process, and so both require a document to inform them as to what is expected on site. (See Fig. 5.3.)

Fig. 5.2 The specification aids accurate tendering

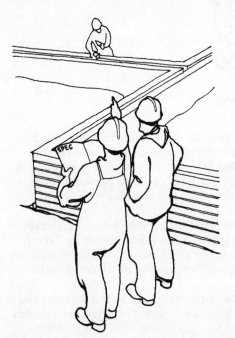

Fig. 5.3 The specification tells the construction team what quality is required

Objectives

For the three purposes referred to, the specification needs to cover a considerable amount of varied information. In particular, it is the only tool available to the designer by which he can readily set out precisely what is required in the following four categories.

1. Extent of the work. Is everything shown on the drawings to be included, or is some existing work, or work to be completed by others shown for clarity's sake? Do the drawings show only the first phase of a more extensive scheme, for which the opportunity to tender may be provided later?
2. The materials to be used, the standards of quality which will be expected, and the means that will be employed to ensure that they are reached.
3. The standards of workmanship that will be demanded, including any guarantees and sanctions to ensure that they are complied with.
4. The conditions under which the work has to be carried out, including time scale, staging of payments, responsibilities of the Contractor, and the form of contract to be used.

None of these items could be unambiguously described on the drawings except in the form of unmanageably copious notes, but the specification can set them out in an easily-read and understood form, provided it is systematically prepared.

Characteristics of the specification

If the specification is to be as useful as possible it must possess certain characteristics. It must be:

(a) *Concise*. It should contain nothing redundant or repetitive. There is no virtue in a long specification for its own sake, and the writer should examine every sentence to ensure that every word is necessary to the proper expression of his intentions.
(b) *Precise*. It should not be capable of misinterpretation. This is a high ambition, and consideration of the wealth of litigation that flows from even the most carefully drafted Acts of Parliament makes one realise how apparently impossible of fulfilment it is. None the less, writers should recognise that if a second interpretation is available the builder will be bound to find it. His aim must be to write a clear and unambiguous statement of his intentions, which clearly evokes an exact picture of what is required.
(c) *Complete*. The reader should not be left with unanswered questions.
(d) *Logical*. The layout should be straightforward and easy to use. No odd clauses should be tucked away in unexpected places where

they may be missed. It is highly desirable that the Standard
Method of Measurement (SMM6) should be followed as to the
order of clauses.

(e) *Complementary*. It must agree with the drawings and schedules,
and should desirably be cross-referenced to them.

In order to convey explicit and complete information, the writer
must of course have arrived at a reasoned decision as to what he
expects in every instance. Every word that is included must be there
for a purpose. He must ask himself whether it is needed, whether it is
the term that most accurately conveys his meaning and whether it can
be misunderstood.

The specification does not lay down HOW work is to be done, but
describes what is to be achieved and the conditions under which this
must be carried out. It is very important that the writer keeps this
principle clearly in mind, or else he may fall into the trap of telling the
builder his job – and of taking upon himself the Contractor's
responsibility for sound building. The writer needs the grounding in
technology that informs him of what is and what is not technically
feasible, and allows him to define the limits of what he requires. He
must be concerned always to describe the end-result rather than the
means of achievement. It is possible, however, that circumstances may
arise in which the best way of describing his requirements is to say that
the work is to be equal to that which could be attained by a particular
technique, or to refer to acceptable samples which are available for
inspection.

Specification-writing is, therefore, a slow and thoughtful task
requiring great clarity of mind, and which must be meticulously carried
out. It is not a job that can readily be delegated.

Writing the specification

Each clause of the specification, as well as each section, should be set
out in a standard way, working from the general to the particular. First
the subject should be identified, then the circumstances should be
described, followed by a description and finally (where this is not clear
from the drawings) by a reference to size.

The language which is employed needs to be selected with care.
There is little to commend legalistic terminology chosen because it
sounds stern and official, and little need for the kind of prose that
avoids punctuation. Words which are in everyday use should be chosen
in preference to abstruse ones, where their meaning is sufficiently
exact: few readers will look-up the unfamiliar term, they will tend
rather to guess at its meaning, and may get it wildly wrong. It is
generally better to refer to a 'property' than to a 'demesne', and to
avoid terms with closely defined legal meanings such as 'enjoyment'.
Technical terms of the construction industry will, of course, abound.

They will carry their normally accepted meaning unless they are specifically defined. This has the effect that if a term carries a 'local' meaning, as is common in the industry, it should be avoided or carefully defined.

Woolly terms, such as 'best quality' or 'to the satisfaction of the Architect' should be regarded as completely unacceptable. Instead precise statements of the standards required must be established, and these should incorporate a definition of the tests or comparisons that will be employed to ensure that they are being achieved.

It is a helpful technique to jot down draft specification clauses as the design evolves, and while the critical factors are clearly in mind. If each clause is inscribed on a separate piece of paper, these can later be juggled into a coherent order to produce the complete specification.

It may be possible to collect standard specification clauses which make the precise demands required. In any case, such clauses may provide a useful starting point for the preparation of new and more particular ones. A bank of such clauses is useful provided their limitations are understood. Any such clause needs to be examined rigorously before it is adopted for re-use, to ensure that it does completely fulfil the designer's intentions.

The usual practice in building-up a bank of standard clauses is to select clauses which have proved successful in practice and to have

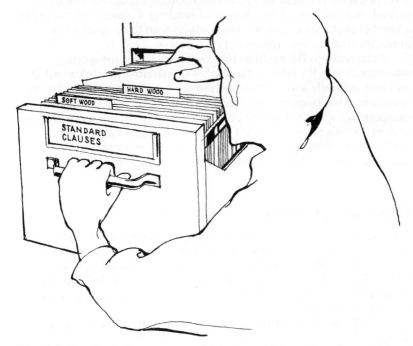

Fig. 5.4 Standard clauses are useful but must be employed carefully

these typed on to index cards. These can then be withdrawn (provided they are properly indexed) evaluated against a new set of circumstances, juggled and retyped as may be necessary. (See Fig. 5.4.)

The use of a computer, especially in association with a word processor, facilitates the process, which appears increasingly attractive and is widely advocated. There are two dangers inherent in the use of standard clauses, however, that need to be recognised and allowed for. One is that because they are neatly typed out and stored they acquire an apparent authority that may be spurious. The other is that it is essential for the bank to be kept systematically up-to-date and regularly revised, which is a daunting task for the smaller practice.

British Standards

Reference to British Standards and British Standard Codes of Practice is useful and economical where these are relevant. It is common to include a preliminary clause which states 'All relevant British Standards and British Standard Codes of Practice are to apply'. This may not of itself, however, ensure that the standards envisaged by the designer will be obtained. If his requirement was in fact for a higher level of excellence than set out in the Standard the clause would, indeed, militate against his chances of reaching it, since there would be a conflict in the specification, and conflicts tend to be resolved by application of the less rigorous of two clauses.

References to BS ought to be to specific clauses for specific instances. Some BS refer to the quality of materials or workmanship and may schedule several standards which are applicable to different situations. Others refer to the detailed design and construction of components, while yet others do little more than set out a classification system. British Standard Codes of Practice include, among other topics, both design and general guidelines: it is important to ensure that references to them are both relevant and specific.

Preliminary clauses

The important preliminary clauses in any specification delineate the scope of what has to be done and the context in which the work has to be carried out. It is imperative that such matters should be described comprehensively, as otherwise the competitiveness of the tendering is jeopardised, and the way will be opened for a plethora of claims for extras during construction.

These clauses are likely to have to cover at least the following topics:

(a) *Scope of the work*. It is highly desirable to start with a succinct statement of the range and scope of the work to be undertaken, in order that the rest of the specification can be understood.

(b) *Place*. A description of the geographical location of the site, with the means of access, space available for storage, huts and parking is needed. Where special measures are needed to ensure the security of the site the conditions (but not the means to be taken) should be described. It is usual and desirable to place an obligation upon tenderers to visit and inspect the site, so that they cannot later claim ignorance of the physical conditions under which the work has to be carried out.

(c) *Time*. Any imperative starting or finishing dates or periods available for construction must be clearly stated, and if such dates are to be conditions of the contract this must be drawn to tenderers' attention. There must also be a description of any sanctions to be adopted to ensure compliance with such conditions.

(d) *Supervision*. The tenderer must be informed under whose supervision the work is to be carried out. He will also require to know how rapidly he can expect the Architect or Clerk of Works to visit the site when their presence is requested, so that he can allow for any consequent delays and the expense they might cause.

(e) *Responsibilities*. The responsibility of the Contractor for every person and thing on the site during construction needs to be defined, especially if the site will be used by others during that period, or existing buildings, planting or other features have to be protected.

(f) *Available facilities*. The tenderer needs to know whether water, drainage or power is available on the site, or whether he must make his own arrangements for temporary services. It is also usual to set out details of any huts, telephone or other facilities which the Contractor must provide for the use of the design team or Clerk of Works, though he is left to determine for himself what huts his own organisation will require.

(g) *Disbursements*. It is essential to point out that the builder must include for all incidental payments, such as holidays with pay, overtime, insurances and so on. It is also highly desirable to specify, if good-quality work is required, that workmen should be paid time rates and not by bonus.

(h) *Payments*. Cash flow is vitally important to the builder, as described in Chapter 8, and it is important for him to know at what intervals he may expect to receive stage payments, what retention fund will be operated, whether half-retention will be released at practical completion and the length of the maintenance period.

(i) *Completion*. The state in which the entire site is to be left at practical completion has to be defined, particularly with regard to the removal of debris from the site.

(j) *Variations*. It would be a very unusual contract in which the completed building agreed completely with that envisaged by the tender documents. Changes are bound to arise because unforeseen (and often unforeseeable) conditions force them upon the team. There must be some predetermined manner in which their cost can be evaluated. In the absence of a schedule of rates it is necessary to invite the Contractor to submit a price for every variation, whether it is an omission or an extra, before the instruction can be given. This can be both time-consuming and expensive.

If extensive remeasurement is anticipated a special schedule should always be drawn-up and priced to form a basis for such valuations. It should be pointed out that the common practice of using the priced Bill of Quantities as a schedule of rates is generally deprecated and of dubious morality.

(k) *Provisional sums*. Provisional sums are used to make sure that money is included in estimates or tenders to cover work which will, it is expected, be complete by the General Contractor but which it is not yet possible to describe in detail.

One might be used, for example, to cover expenditure in connection with a plaque to be unveiled at the opening ceremony.

It is also appropriate to use such a sum in cases where alteration work is being undertaken, and it is impossible to determine in advance how much of an existing structure needs to be replaced or perhaps the extent of damage that might be found. In new work the nature of the ground might make it impossible to design foundations in detail until excavations had begun, and a provisional sum could be used.

An alternative strategy in such circumstances is to include precise instructions for the work but to indicate that the whole of that section of the drawings and specification is 'provisional' and subject to later remeasurement against an agreed schedule of rates.

A provisional sum should not be used in any case simply to avoid early preparation of details. Everything which CAN be finalised before tender stage SHOULD be. This is not only so that the estimator has an accurate idea of what is required but also essential because of the interdependence of so many parts of any scheme. For example, it is not unknown for preparation of a paving layout to be left for completion near the time when pavings will be laid–towards the end of the contract. It may then be found that constraints imposed by the drainage, completed long before, prevent a preferred design, and limit the options available.

(l) *Contingency sum*. An important provisional sum which is almost always necessary is the 'contingency sum'. This is present so that there will be a reserve of money available to cover any genuinely unexpected and necessary work. It is not there to cover the items the Architect forgot about or extra extravagances either he or the

Client would like to include. If no unpredicted work has been required, the unspent contingency sum will provide a pleasant unexpected saving for the client.

The first Architect's Instruction generally omits the provisional sums *en bloc*, and expenditure against them is made one by one through the Architect's Instructions in due course.

(m) *Prime Cost (PC) Sums.* Prime cost sums are included to cover work to be carried out by nominated subcontractors, and to the cost of which the Contractor is rightly entitled to add percentages to cover profit and attendances.

Where it is possible, it is often preferable to obtain subcontract tenders before tenders for the general contract are invited, so that the whole of the details can be finalised. Where this is done the work in question can be included as a measured or described item and the financial uncertainty associated with the use of PC sums is eliminated.

Clauses describing particular materials

Quality

The grades and quality of each material which is to be used must be set out. Where there is an appropriate British Standard this should of course, be referred to. Otherwise, care should be taken to state the defects which will lead to rejection (including faulty storage and use), as well as particular features which are required, such as regularity. Where comparison will be made with an acceptable sample, this should be available at tender stage for inspection if ambiguity is to be avoided.

Tests

The specification should also include a description of the tests which will be applied (including submission to independent laboratories) and the level of results that will be required.

Source

Where the source of a material is considered significant – as it might be either to ensure a proper match with existing work or because the Client insisted on business being done with particular firms or countries – this must be clearly stated. To impose such a condition at a later stage would quite reasonably lead to a claim from the Contractor for reimbursement of additional expenditure incurred as a result.

Manufacturer

Where a proprietary material is selected, it is reasonable firstly to obtain the advice of the manufacturer on its use, so as to include his recommendations in the specification, and secondly to refer the Contractor to him for guidance. Manufacturers are generally most willing to provide this back-up to sales, as they wish to see their products effectively used and to build-up their reputation for reliable products.

There has been considerable debate on the extent to which the naming of particular manufacturers in specifications prevents truly competitive tendering. Some specifiers prefer to include meticulously detailed descriptions of the materials or fittings in question, in the hope that these can then be obtained from truly competitive sources. This is rarely the case. On occasions it is found that the article so carefully described is not in fact on the market, and though no doubt industry is willing to develop it, the consequent delay is unacceptable. Another pitfall is that the description so perfectly fits an individual product that competition is no more likely than if the labour-saving device of naming the firm and catalogue number had been chosen.

An option which is sometimes found acceptable is to specify an item as 'at least equal to Messrs So-and-So's catalogue number x in all respects'. This does allow a competitor to offer his product.

All in all, however, there seems little doubt that to collect information on a wide range of products from which one selects for particular cases is a generally satisfactory procedure. The designer should avoid always specifying the products of the same firm, and must be ready to listen receptively to the blandishments of other manufacturers' representatives.

Individual elements

The specification clauses which describe particular elements must be arranged in a logical sequence, as has already been described. This process is often easiest if the writer imagines himself explaining what is needed to the site agent or trade foreman in a face-to-face situation. The recipient of oral information would be able to ask questions to clarify doubtful points, and such questions must be anticipated and forestalled in a written description.

In a conversation, one would begin by stating the subject to be described and where it fitted into the building, going on to talk about material, quality and size before going into more detailed points. This must be done in writing, too.

Name
It is essential to start by naming the element. This may require some precision. If there are several types of window, each will be separately described, and the description must begin by identifying which is being dealt with.

Location

The second requisite for clarity is to locate the element in relation to the remainder of the building, so that it is understood in context by the reader.

Drawings

Since drawings and specification are complementary, the next step should be to identify the drawings against which the description is to be read. Size should be shown on the drawing, and ought not, therefore, to be referred to in the specification. Duplicated information is always liable to conflicts and errors. If it is felt necessary to include size in the description it should be made clear that the sizes included in the specification are nominal and for identification only, and that actual sizes should be obtained from the drawings (which may, of course, in turn refer to the need to check actual working sizes on sites). (See Fig. 5.5.)

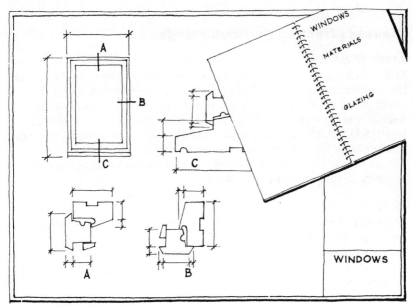

Fig. 5.5 The specification describes those matters which cannot be shown on the drawings

Materials

The materials to be used should next be described, as discussed above, including descriptions of quality and tests as may be appropriate.

Finish

Where a particular standard of finish is required, some care should be taken in choosing the words in which this is specified. It is not usually satisfactory to refer to the standard obtained by skilled workmen, or to 'good' quality. Reference to an acceptable sample which is available for inspection by tenderers is better.

Appearance

It will rarely be necessary to include specific references to appearance in specifications, though unacceptable blemishes will be described under 'Quality'.

Tolerances

Plus and minus tolerances of size in relation to nominal or site-measured sizes often need to be set out, particularly in the case of dry construction (see Ch. 15). The Contractor should be left in no doubt that components showing an unacceptable range of variation will be rejected.

Clauses affecting particular trades

Trade practices

Many trades embrace traditional practices hallowed by time, but which the Architect may dislike. In such a case, special mention should be made of the point in the trade preambles. For example, floor-tilers normally make a practice of setting-out tiles from the centre of each room, while Architects may prefer to have uncut tiles running through doorways, or tiles laid out in some other way in strict accordance with the drawings. This will not be done without extra cost unless attention is drawn to the point at tender stage.

Skill

The level of skill, training or experience of tradesmen is described by some specifiers where particularly high standards are required. This may appear reasonable, but is unpopular with builders and unions, and it should be avoided unless there are especially important grounds for its introduction.

The performance specification

There is considerable controversy surrounding the use of the performance specification on any widespread scale.

On the one hand, stand many designers who believe that contractors should be told what final result is required but not how it is to be achieved. They hold that a builder's expertise can be most readily tapped by describing for him, precisely, all the requirements of a component while leaving other features which are not critical to his discretion. What is critical will vary with the particular case, but this might include size, tolerance, U-value, colour and finish and weight while not extending to the material to be used nor its method of manufacture.

Many Contractors, on the other hand, feel that such a stance is an abdication of responsibility by the designer, and that the risk involved in trying to fulfil a performance specification at minimum cost is one they ought not to be asked to shoulder. They contend, too, that the scrupulous firm which includes in its tender price for a fully adequate response to such a specification is liable to find the contract awarded to a less responsible builder who hopes to creep through the wording of the clause with minimum cover.

In spite of the conflict between these views, much specialised work has in fact been carried out for many years by way of performance specification. The secret appears to lie in a very precise statement of mandatory requirements and an equally clear definition of which matters are left to the Contractor's discretion.

In the case of a roof covering, for example, the specification may call quite simply for a system guaranteed to remain watertight for a given period. Maximum fall, maximum weight and a possible colour requirement would commonly be the only other parameters given. The Contractor would be left to decide on the materials to be used, the allowance to be made for movement, the need to insulate or ventilate the screed and so on. A firm marketing a proprietary system would welcome such as opportunity, though many contractors would be reluctant to tender under similar terms for walling or other structural parts of a building.

It is reasonable to allow the specialist manufacturer of a security system, an escalator or curtain-walling at least to propose the details of what should be included, and this extends to most fields with which an Architect would usually expect to have limited experience. The Architect must, however, maintain his role of balancing the demands of a team of specialists to obtain the optimum total response to his Client's needs, and the specialist manufacturer should never be in the position of dictating overall design.

A 'master list' of the properties of materials relevant to building which assists the exact definition of requirements, can be obtained from the Secretariat of the International Council for Building Research, (CIB) P.O. Box 299, Rotterdam, The Netherlands (CIB report No. 3).

Chapter 6

Quality control

Establishing an acceptable level of quality ought to be a cooperative venture between the design and construct teams. The Contractor has an interest in preserving his reputation for producing fine work, and should be encouraged to display the ability of his craftsmen to the best advantage.

However, the Contractor has a duty to maximise the return to his shareholders, and is for this reason under pressure to produce the cheapest building he can. It is not to be wondered at if this sometimes results in attempts to cut corners where he believes this to be unimportant. Undoubtedly, too, there are unscrupulous firms who will attempt to get away with inferior materials and workmanship where they believe they can do so undetected.

One factor which militates heavily against high quality is the payment of bonuses for quantity of production. Workmen are naturally averse to losing their bonus because of having to work more carefully (and so slowly) than they feel they could. If their hasty work is rejected they may be equally recalcitrant. Where high quality is required it is often felt to be advisable to specify that payment should be by time rates to avoid this problem.

The specification, which is discussed in detail in Chapter 5, sets out results to be achieved but not the means by which this should be done. It will usually refer to British Standards and British Standard Codes of Practice, which in turn indicate acceptable levels of quality and standard tests by which these can be established. This is not in itself a sufficient guarantee that satisfactory results will ensue.

Careful supervision of work on site is essential if the quality specified – and tendered for – is to be reached. The attainment of such levels of excellence can, however, be fostered by certain conditions.

(a) The quality specified should be of a level which is realistic and reasonable in the particular circumstances. In any case where an unusually high standard is set, the fact should be clearly drawn to the attention of tenderers. If, for example, standards of joinery more usually associated with commercial work were being called for in housing, this may not be appreciated by estimaters unless the circumstance is pointed out. A failure to recognise such a point would lead to underpricing, and later to difficulties and potential dispute of site. As discussed in Chapter 5, the specification should not require a standard higher than will actually be expected. Equally, site control must not demand standards above those of the specification.

(b) Only firms known to be capable of producing work of the required standard should be invited to tender. The practice of some authorities in inviting open tenders is to be deprecated from this viewpoint, and can lead to endless site difficulties. Firms, too, which are known to pay more attention to making a quick profit than to their reputation ought to be avoided where high quality is needed. Although a firm continues to carry responsibility for its work after completion, it should not be forgotten that it is easy to escape from such commitments by going out of business.

(c) The appointment of a Clerk of Works of demonstrable competence is essential, and he should also possess qualities of personality which allow him to supervise and perhaps guide without becoming autocratic. He should aim to get the cooperation of the builder rather than to enter into a battle of wits with him.

(d) It is extremely important to establish a good working relationship with the builder, based on recognition of shared goals and mutual respect. With his reputation at stake, the builder should be expected to be anxious to provide what is necessary – although he must naturally do so as efficiently as possible. So long as he understands clearly what is required of him and there is no attempt to tell him HOW that should be managed, he is normally glad to be cooperative.

(e) The standard which will be required should be explained clearly at the commencement of the job, so that there is no subsequent confusion on this score. Any dispute as to the interpretation of the specification should also be resolved at this stage. The Contractor and the craftsmen need to be clear to which points the greatest importance is attached, on which points the supervisors may be open to discussion, and perhaps about the personal quirks and prejudices of the design and supervision team. In the absence of such guidance they may be forgiven for assuming that some practice which has been tacitly accepted elsewhere will pass muster when this is not in fact the case.

(f) Local authority inspections should not be relied on to indicate satisfactory or unsatisfactory work. They will be limited to matters covered by the Building Regulations, and may be satisfied by lower standards than those required by the specification.

Site visits

During regular site inspections a check is, of course, kept on the rate of progress of the work compared to the expectations of the builder as set out in his detailed programme.

This is also the major opportunity afforded to designers to establish that the specified quality is being provided. A number of general observations will provide a context for more detailed examination.

Tidiness of site

The general attitude of the builder and his workforce to their work is demonstrated by the organisation and tidiness of the site. There ought to be a general absence of litter, and particularly of discarded materials – on the other hand, an excessive zeal for tidiness might well be thought of as misdirected energy.

Safety

The safety of the site is, of course, the responsibility of the builder. None the less, attention to the guarding of scaffolding, the use of protective clothing and so on is an indication of a responsible attitude, which is likely to permeate other aspects of the builder's work.

Storage of materials

The supervisor should be alert to see that materials on site are stored under suitable conditions and protected from the ground and from the weather where this is important. They should be separated from one another.

There should be an adequate supply of materials on site to avoid delays, but not an excess. Materials delivered too soon may be unnecessarily exposed both to deterioration and to pilfering.

Protection of completed work

It should be evident that the Contractor is taking care to protect completed work from damage by following trades, and this should include both the use of protective coverings and the completion of the most vulnerable elements at as late a stage as possible in the contract.

Weather

The work should continue only in suitable weather conditions, depending on the operation in question, unless special precautions are taken. Such precautions (the incorporation of anti-freeze in concrete, for example) should only be employed if they are allowed for in the specification and agreed by the Architect.

Details

Care should be taken to ensure that the details are being followed in every respect. Should site circumstances require a change of detail, this should be discussed and agreed by the Architect before any relevant work is put in hand. It is generally inadvisable to approve such changes immediately on site. The proposal should be considered, with all its implications, unhurriedly in the office before a decision is given.

Individual points

Excavation and foundations

Irrespective of the depth of topsoil shown on the drawings, it is vital to ensure that the whole of the vegetable soil has been removed from the building area, and separately stacked.

Foundation trenches must be taken down at least to the levels shown on the drawings, and deeper if pockets of dubious bearing capacity are found. The sides of trenches must be adequately supported so that soil does not collapse into and contaminate concrete, and all trenches should be kept clear of water until foundations are complete. (See Fig. 6.1)

The hardcore should be inspected to ensure that it is free from

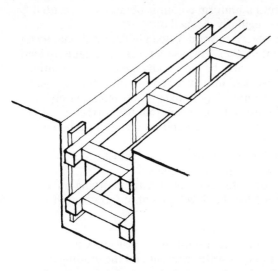

Fig. 6.1 The earth in foundation trenches should be supported

organic matter, and that the blinding is clean and well compacted. Correct placing of DPCs and membranes, with proper laps, should be monitored, and especially attention paid to avoiding perforations of the DPM.

At completion, a check should be made to ensure that the DPC is everywhere a minimum of 150 mm above ground level, and unobstructed by flower-beds or pavings.

Concrete

Although concrete is so commonly used a material as to become routine, this should not be allowed to lead to any slackening in the meticulous care needed in its production if quality is to be maintained.

Visual examination of the materials is helpful, especially if it can include comparison with accepted samples. Cement should be dry, floury and free from lumps, while sand should not be clayey, and should neither cohere into lumps nor stain the hands. There should be no visible organic matter, and no scum should form on the surface of a sample immersed in water.

It is critical that materials should be properly stored. Cement should be kept in watertight containers and used in rotation, and aggregates should be separated and kept clear of the soil. The moisture content of aggregates must be taken into account in determining the quantity of water to be added to the mix to obtain the specified water – cement ratio (see Ch. 2) and this may necessitate regular testing of samples for water content.

Materials should be accurately batched by weight where possible, and the equipment used needs to be tested (including the water valve) from time to time.

Adequate mixing until a uniform colour is obtained is essential, and the mixer should be regularly cleaned out.

Concrete should be placed only on a clean bed, and should never be dropped from a height of over 1 m, as that would be liable to lead to segregation of the mix. It may be worked by hand or by vibration, so long as it is carefully worked into every corner of formwork, and between reinforcement. Consolidation must follow immediately.

Inspection should be made to ascertain that the correct reinforcement is being correctly placed and protected from being dislodged during pouring.

Daywork joints need to be carefully made against exposed aggregate, in order to ensure an adequate key.

The slow curing of concrete prevents over-rapid drying out of the water, which is needed for the development of full strength.

Slump test

The slump test, shown in Fig. 6.2, establishes consistency in the concrete being poured so far as water content and the grading of

Fig. 6.2 The slump test

aggregate are concerned, and gives a good index of workability. The results are immediately available.

Test cubes

The strength of concrete is measured by standardised crushing tests on 150-mm cubes, but since these tests are made at intervals of up to twenty-eight days the results do not give immediate feedback. Figure

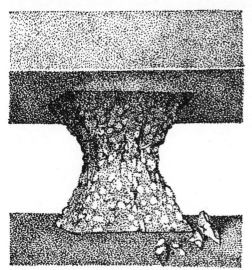

Fig. 6.3 Crushing test on concrete cube

6.3 shows the test. Some specifications provide for the testing of cores cut from the material placed on site, where a cube fails to develop the required strength after the full allowed period.

Formwork

Formwork should be clean and accurately made and placed, with sufficient support to avoid undue deflection during placement of the concrete. It should be well oiled before every use.

Screeds and floor finishes

Where screeds are indicated, they should be laid either on green concrete or in thicker form on concrete which has been mechanically keyed. They should be truly level, which can most easily be tested with a rolling marble. Where conduits run through screed, they should be bridged by reinforcement.

Expansion joints may be needed to allow for differential movement in terrazzo or granolithic floors, and hardwood-block floors should incorporate sufficient cork expansion joints to take up movement due to changes in moisture content. (See Fig. 6.4)

Accuracy in placing the joints in tiled floors greatly enhances the appearance of the rooms.

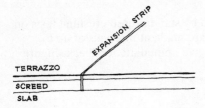

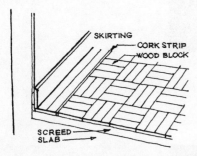

Fig. 6.4 Expansion joints to finishes

Brickwork

The materials for mortar should be stored in comparable conditions to those for concrete (see above). Bricks should be carefully unloaded and stacked (never tipped) or may be delivered paletted.

Sample bricks should be deposited and approved and subsequent deliveries compared with the approved sample. Accuracy of shape and the absence of cracks and other damage should be assessed. Samples can be tested for porosity by comparing dry with saturated weight. This is not, however, considered to give a reliable index of durability, and where frost damage is considered potentially likely the manufacturer should be asked to provide frost-resistant bricks, which he can show to have withstood extreme exposure. Where strength is critical, samples should be submitted for crushing test.

Checks should be made to ensure that brickwork is plumb, that it is rising steadily with an even (usually specified) number of courses to the metre, and that it does not rise more than eight courses per day. Particular care should be taken to check the accuracy of quoins. The vertical joints, known as perpends, should be vertically above one another. (See Fig. 6.5.)

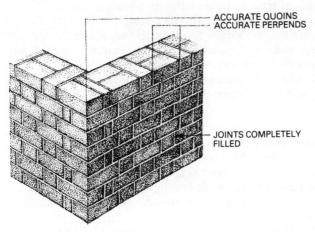

ACCURATE QUOINS
ACCURATE PERPENDS

JOINTS COMPLETELY
FILLED

Fig. 6.5 Quality in brickwork

There should be no mortar deposits or stains on the face of brickwork. If these are found and builder offers to clean them he should be invited to demonstrate that this can be done satisfactorily without damage to the bricks before such a practice is authorised. Otherwise the brickwork should be taken down and rebuilt. The mortar colour should be consistent, all the joints should be completely filled and neatly finished to the agreed style. If pointing is specified, joints should be cleanly raked out before pointing proceeds, and the pointing should be continuous and in carefully-controlled pointing mortar. Frogs must be filled, and there must be no mortar droppings in cavities, a cavity board being used.

In dry weather clay bricks should be wetted before use and

previous work wetted before work continues, to avoid excessive suction.

Green brickwork should be protected from frost.

Mortar must be well mixed dry before being mixed while water is added. It should be made in small quantities and used at once.

Work should be checked to ascertain that ties, DPCs, cavity trays and lintols are being correctly placed.

Timber

Structural

Timber should be stored in conditions of humidity similar to those in which it is to be used, in order to protect the moisture content. That which has been pressure-impregnated with preservative should have been saturated, and this is most easily monitored if a coloured material has been used.

Material should be inspected visually to ensure that it is straight in grain and generally in accordance with the specification where regularity and the absence of knots are concerned.

Joists and other members must be accurately set out and adequately seated, and joints should fit snugly. Connectors should only be used where specified or by previous agreement.

No timber should be built into any fireplace or flue. The work must follow the details in all respects.

Joinery

Softwood.   Joinery should be delivered to site primed, so that it is generally necessary to visit the shop to inspect the components during manufacture to ensure that material as specified is being used.

Joints should be accurately made and tightly fitted, and care should be taken to see that they do not provide pockets where water can lodge, encouraging rot.

The finish should be careful and smooth, arrises should be consistent and to an agreed pattern, and the details should be followed in all respects.

Hardwood.   Much of what is said above under softwood applies.

Hardwood joinery should use timber which matches agreed samples and be free from visible defects. If filling is acceptable, the colour must match that of the wood.

Surface dampening of the wood will indicate what the polished colour will be, without staining.

Fittings

All doors and windows should open and close smoothly, and all furniture should be checked to see that it works correctly and is neatly fitted, as well as being of the specified material and pattern.

Roof

The sarking should be inspected to ensure that it is tucked into gutters, and flashings should be checked to see that they are properly wedged.

Plaster

All plaster should have a true face (which can be checked by rotating a batten on the surface) and should not be overworked, but show a uniform texture. In two-coat work, the first coat should be scratched to provide a key.

Plaster should be tapped – if a hollow ring is heard, the adhesion is suspect. Adhesion to old brickwork or concrete may be aided by the use of a proprietary bonder.

Care should be taken to ensure that all beads or Keene's cement arrises have been incorporated where specified.

Skirtings and architraves should be fixed to grounds after plastering, and there should be no gaps between the back of such cover strips and the plaster face. Cornices should not be fixed to both wall and ceiling, as shown in Fig. 6.6.

The joints of plasterboard and the bridges over conduit should be scrimmed to reinforce the plaster, as shown in Fig. 6.7.

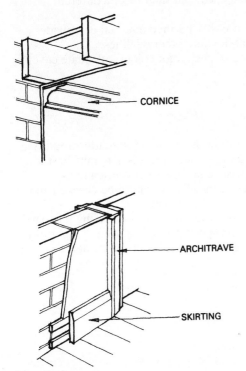

Fig. 6.6 Trim fixed to one face only

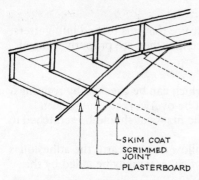

Fig. 6.7 Scrim reinforcement to plaster

Paintwork

The method of application of paint should be a matter for the Contractor's decision, provided he can demonstrate a satisfactory final result.

Generally more acceptable results come from multiple coats than from single-coat paint systems, and to ensure that every coat has been applied it is usual to specify that each coat shall be of a different colour.

The painter should either use the specified material or provide evidence of at least equal durability and other qualities.

Finished surfaces should be inspected for colour, adequate cover and uniform texture.

General

It has been possible only to mention the commonest matters requiring site supervision here. When making a site visit it is generally best to consult the programme and the specification in advance and to makeup a brief schedule of the items which ought to be checked and any tests or observations which should be made.

What is most critical will vary with the conditions of the job. The supervisor should assume that the specification has been thoughtfully written, and that his task is to ensure that it is fully implemented.

Chapter 7

Planned maintenance

Relationship between maintenance and design

We are sometimes told that the manufacturers of consumer goods aim to have all the parts wear out at a given time, so that the entire apparatus is no longer repairable, but must be replaced. Since they often fail to maintain stocks of spares after a similar period, there appears to be some evidence in support of such a suggestion. The 'principle' has been labelled 'built-in obsolesence' – and is actually supposed to include the incorporation of stylistic motifs which will date, to encourage the consumer to buy new, to maximise the market, and so to cheapen the goods.

It must surely be rare for such a system to be adopted in the case of buildings – though American office blocks are demolished rather than adapted after quite a short span of life. None the less, there are two contrasted approaches to their maintenance, one of which owes something to the philosophy described.

Maintenance in perfect condition

In the first of these, the aim of maintenance is seen to be keeping the building in the condition in which it was originally handed over. This means that at the end of its intended life the owner will be left with an asset with a considerable resale value. The cost of maintenance to such a standard is likely to increase progressively as the building ages. It should also be noted that even if the original standards are meticulously preserved, the building will not continue to give the original standard of satisfaction: as it becomes possible to provide higher and higher standards, so these become enmeshed in users' expectations. For example, if an hotel were built to '3-star' standards, and well kept (from the housekeeping as well as from the management point of view) it might nevertheless slip down the star ratings because the specifications for those ratings rose. To maintain 3-star status, and be able to continue to charge accordingly, it could be necessary to make actual, and expensive, improvements.

Controlled deterioration

The alternative approach is to aim at a building which is fit only for demolition at the end of its planned life, but has had the minimum spent on it meanwhile.

In this case the hotel would be allowed to slip gradually down the ratings, no doubt to end its life as a common dosshouse. This approach has parallels with the 'built-in obsolescence' referred to previously.

Comparison

The example of an hotel is significant, because it is immediately apparent that the charges a hotelier can make are directly related to the status – and therefore the state – of his premises. One expects to pay more for a room in a 3-star establishment than in a 2-star one. The calculation has to take into account not only the anticipated expenditure and the residual value of the investment, but the expected revenue, too.

The decision is a difficult commercial one, based on the application of terotechnology (see Ch. 8), and it is not one to which the designer should normally expect to contribute. He may well be asked to provide data and advice which will help the investor to make up his mind, however, and once a decision has been taken it is imperative to recognise this as one of the parameters governing the design solution, with an established order of priority. The financial calculations are basic to the commerical viability of the project, and must be respected: to do otherwise would be irresponsible.

The final decision will, of course, normally lie somewhere between the two extremes described.

Minimising maintenance costs

It is self-evident that standards of maintenance will be highest where there is an unlimited budget: this is a rare occurrence! It is generally essential that what sums are available are spent to the greatest possible advantage, and the most significant influences in retarding deterioration are undoubtedly the care and thought paid to maintenance problems at the design stage. This can be applied in two principal ways as follows.

Elimination of avoidable maintenance

A very great deal can be done to reduce the amounts needing to be spent year after year on repairs, replacements and redecoration by careful detailing and thoughtful selection of materials.

Resistant materials

It is a sensible strategy to select materials which will resist the kinds of environmental attack which is to be expected in the particular vicinity. For example, in a seaside location care should be taken to avoid materials liable to corrosion in salt-laden air, like steel, while in an industrial atmosphere silicaceous or ferruginous rather than calcareous sandstone might be used as it is less liable to blistering due to sulphurous acids in the air. All details ought to be scrutinised to ensure that no potential cause of deterioration has been built in to the proposals.

Durable materials

In any case it is sound sense to prefer durable materials which do not require continual attention, and particularly those whose corrosion is self-limiting, like copper. This may well be an expensive initial expedient, but will inevitably show benefits if cost-in-use calculations are made.

Protection

Areas which are particularly vulnerable to attack (such as doors through which trolleys are pushed, or plaster arrises) should be specifically designed so that damage is minimised. Such doors can be of the flexible type, or be protected by metal plates (and probably also require view panels, for the protection of people coming the other way) while vulnerable plaster arrises should be protected by wooden or metal beads.

Limitation of paintwork

The temptation to paint every surface in sight which apparently afflicts some designers ought to be rigorously resisted: once painted, any surface requires regular and expensive attention. No surface should be painted unless this is necessary either for:
(a) Protection (as in the case of steel or softwood).
(b) Genuine decorative reasons (plastered walls).

Paint system

The protective purpose of a paint film is usually fulfilled by a system consisting of:
(a) Meticulous surface preparation to ensure good adhesion. This may include degreasing or etching with mordant solution, and proper knotting and stopping of timber.

(b) Selection of a primer compatible with the material to be decorated.

(c) Undercoats which are opaque and sufficiently flexible to provide a durable protection through minor movements.

(d) A top coat chosen for durability under the conditions of exposure anticipated.

Paintwork needs attention when:

(a) There is any sign of blistering or flaking, in which case the surface should be cleaned of all loose material, filled and redecorated.

(b) Saponification, flashing or other defects listed in Chapter 2 are present.

(c) Colours fade or darken so as to make an appreciable change in the appearance and (in the case of interiors) to the distribution of light.

The whole paint system should be removed only when it is so seriously faulty that remedial work would be more expensive than removal and renewal, or when so many coats have been applied that detail is obscured. Otherwise, the surface should be rubbed down and any deficiencies filled before the application of one or more new coats over the old, which continue to serve a protective purpose.

When it is essential to remove the entire system, chemical strippers should generally be preferred to the more hazardous blowtorch, which can damage glass and timber extensively in careless hands.

Permanent coatings

Whether paintwork is considered for a decorative or a protective reason, the method and materials chosen will be the same, and regular redecoration will be necessary.

In either case, a permanent coating should be preferred to a paint system wherever this can be afforded, because over the lifetime of the building the cost of redecoration, including the inconvenience and the costs of having accommodation out of use, are likely to be disproportionately large.

The only disadvantage to permanent coatings is that the colours cannot be changed. In buildings where regular refurbishment is a positive advantage (such as a boutique, perhaps) a different attitude may be preferred, but in general careful selection of colours both for their psychological effect and for the subtle relationships between them should lead to a scheme which neither dates not palls, so that permanent finishes are no disadvantage.

Integral finishes

For similar reasons to those discussed above, the selection of integral finishes is to be encouraged. With these there is little danger of deterioration: they are not even liable to loss of bond, which may afflict even durable applied sheet finishes.

In the case of each of the strategies suggested above, careful cost-in-use calculations should be made, and these will generally be found to show a financial advantage in spending rather more on the original building in order to minimise later costs (including the cost and inconvenience of time out of use) of maintenance. (See Ch. 8.)

Design for good supervision
Vandalism, as well as the careless use of the facilities provided, can be minimised by arranging a building so that there are no unsupervised corners, or safe spots where anti-social behaviour can go on unobserved. This does not mean that constant supervision is essential, but rather that potential hooligans are aware that their activities might at any time be observed.

Encourage a sense of 'belonging'
It is a matter of common observation that people who feel a place is their own, and who take a pride in it, use it with greater care than those who feel it is anonymous. The provision of carpets is said to encourage the proper use of ashtrays and doormats, and consulting users about the way furniture should be arranged, or the colours to be selected, can help them to identify with a building.

An owner usually finds that a high level of housekeeping actually minimises maintenance costs because a building which is seen to be carefully cared for is less likely to be misused.

Facilitation of necessary maintenance
Some maintenance work is, of course, unavoidable. The regular housekeeping aimed at removing dirt is essential, damaged components have to be replaced, and services often need attention. If serious thought is devoted to making such tasks easy the amount of work involved, and the cost, can be considerably reduced. Points which deserve attention include the following.

Access to services
A very early decision should be concerned with the method of access which is to be given to services. Clearly, if crawlways and large accessible vertical ducts can be provided, this allows for work to proceed with a minimum of disruption to the normal use of the building. Unless such crawlways provide genuinely adequate working space, however, so that the necessary tools can be efficiently used, the cramped conditions in which work has to be carried out can make maintenance both inconvenient and expensive. A horizontal crawlway probably needs to have a clear space 900 mm wide × 1 m high to be a possible place to work in. Crawlways can be a security risk.

Wide, shallow ducts with continuous access covers, preferably reached from areas where their use will be unobtrusive (and not from corridors, as is so often the case) make the work of the maintenance crew much easier, and are usually cheaper and simpler to provide. They may, however, be unacceptable in public buildings.

Visibly mounted services are both cheap and easy to get at. If very great care is taken they can be arranged so as to be aesthetically acceptable, and can as reasonably be important elements in the architectural expression as structural elements can. The Pompidou Centre, in Paris, clears the floor space of services by arranging these on the exterior of the building, to magnificient effect, as Fig. 7.1 shows.

Fig. 7.1 Services can be a feature of the design

In any case, it is vital when laying out the services for any building to ensure that one set of pipes does not obscure access to another: ducted service layouts should always be detailed for this reason, and the drawings should usually show the arrangement in three dimensions. The fitters must never be allowed to arrange their services on an *ad hoc*, or first-come first-served basis.

Replacements

It has to be remembered that the life of many components is less than that planned for the whole building. Boilers, tanks or lift motors may have to be replaced, possibly more than once. The cost of renewal will,

of course, be taken into account in the terotechnological calculations.
(See Ch. 8.) In addition it is important that space for manoeuvring
the parts is allowed, and thought is given to the means by which the
weights involved will be handled. If this is not done, considerable
unanticipated costs can be incurred, in removing and rebuilding
structures which are in the way.

Other components of the building may need to be renewed
because they have been damaged. Cladding panels and glass (for
example) should (if at all vulnerable) be detailed so that this can be
done without undue difficulty, and preferably without the need for
scaffolding. On the other hand, of course, such panels must not be so
easily removed from the exterior as to present a security risk.

Easy cleaning
All buildings must be kept clean internally.

This can be made very much easier if shapes are kept simple,
crannies are avoided, and corners are rounded. Housekeeping staff are
supposed to work only at floor level, and not to use step-ladders, so
high ledges should be avoided where this is possible. The use of
corbelled fittings, wall-hung cupboards, and rounded skirtings is to be
encouraged. (See Fig. 7.2.)

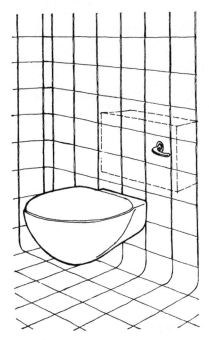

Fig. 7.2 Design to minimise housework

Wash-down surfaces are easier to keep in order than ones which need to be polished, though the two should not be contiguous, else water may damage polished surfaces while polish may damage ones which need to be sluiced. Similarly, vacuum-cleaning is efficient provided it covers large enough areas. A whole space should ideally be arranged so that a minimum number of different cleaning operations is required. Installation of a ducted vacuum system should be discussed with the Client: opinions as to its usefulness vary.

Windows which can be reversed so as to be cleaned from inside the building have much to recommend them above first-floor level since they avoid the need for cradles and probably outside contract cleaners. Their presence may also lead to more regular window-cleaning, since the operation is easier. The system is, however, to some extent controversial, since access to rooms is demanded: the acceptability of this must be determined by the client. (See Fig. 7.3.)

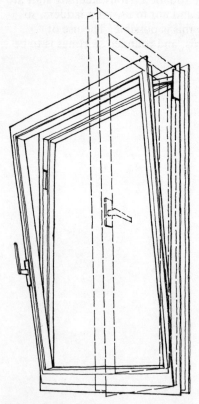

Fig. 7.3 Inside cleaning of windows may be preferred

Handbook

The users of buildings will be helped to keep them in good condition with the least expense and difficulty if they are provided with really adequate information about them. Very commonly, little more than a set of construction drawings (amended to bring them up-to-date) is handed over. Such drawings are confusing and difficult to read for the layman. They include considerable unnecessary information, while information which is essential for this purpose (such as the names and addresses of suppliers) is omitted.

A proper user's handbook (Fig. 7.4.) will provide the following information.

Fig. 7.4 Owner's handbook

(a) Easily read and specially prepared drawings showing the whole building in plan and elevation, preferably related to an axonometric or isometric key.

It has to be remembered that plaster-to-plaster measurements are of more interest to the occupant than structural dimensions. He is also interested in floor and wall areas. The structural parts of the building must be very clearly differentiated to guard against the danger of imprudent removal.

(b) Separate drawings of each service layout are necessary, and in many cases these can most easily be understood by the layman if they are drawn as axonometrics. They must indicate the purpose of every pipe, show stop-taps and draw-off points, and refer to the system of colour coding adopted. It should be immediately apparent to a newcomer seeing the drawing for the first time where a service should be turned-off when a fault occurs: it is not always the regular maintenance staff who are at hand to cope when such circumstances arise. Similarly, the drawing of the electric service must make it immediately clear which main switch and which fuse or circuit-breaker controls which circuits.

(c) Identification of all items of plant should be included. The name and address of the manufacturer, the code name, type and catalogue number of the item, should appear in the main document, with a cross-reference to the manufacturer's handbook or instruction manual, which should be bound in as an appendix.

(d) Similarly, components such as handles, taps and similar fittings which may need to be replaced or repeated should be identified. The manufacturer's name, address and catalogue number, with a description of the finish, as well as the manufacturer's recommendations for cleaning and maintenance should be included.

In the case of locks, a suiting plan will be necessary, and must indicate the mastering pattern, with code numbers, which will allow the ordering of additional locks under the existing suites.

(e) All the materials used as integral or applied finishes need to be identified with some precision. In this case the manufacturer's maintenance recommendations should be stressed, since considerable and expensive damage can be done by the unthinking use of inappropriate cleaning methods.

The name and address of the manufacturer and/or supplier, with the code name or catalogue number and colour of the material should be given. If at all possible (though the information may not be available from the manufacturer for a patented product) the actual composition as well as the trade description of the material should be included.

The colours of paints should be given both by the trade name and by the Munsell or BS code.

(f) Where breakdown of any item might be critical, or where long delivery times for items are to be expected, this should be indicated, with a recommendation that standby stocks should be kept. An indication of the level of such stocks would be helpful.

(g) An indication should be given of the points to which special attention should be paid during regular inspections. The desirability of such inspections to minimise the maintenance work needed, on the analogy of regular visits to the dentist, should be stressed.

While the development of faults is not, of course, anticipated, some description of symptoms which might indicate the need for expert attention, as well as of those (like shrinkage cracks) which are not of serious importance, is reassuring for occupants.

(h) The names, addresses and telephone numbers of the General Contractor and major subcontractors should be given. If the name of a particular person to be contacted can be given this is helpful.

(i) The name, address and telephone number of the Architect, with the name and extension number of the assistant in charge of the job (and if it can be arranged, his home telephone number as well) must be included. Similar information regarding Consultants is discretionary – some Architects will prefer all enquiries to be directed through their own offices.

Maintenance schedule

Figure 7.5 shows a typical maintenance schedule for a simple building.

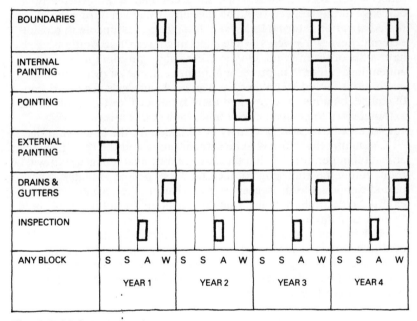

Fig. 7.5 Maintenance chart

Preparation of the maintenance schedule, so as to spread the disturbance and expense of proper care of the building, or alternatively to concentrate this into specific 'off peak' periods, is of course a matter for the owner or occupant. He may, however, seek advice with regard to the regularity with which particular jobs (particularly repainting) are required.

He should be encouraged to make regular systematic inspections of the property. These can be based on specially prepared outline plans, and should ensure that every vulnerable part of the building is inspected for incipient faults, so that these can be attended to before major problems develop. Notes should be kept, so that a record of the development of (say) a sagging beam or damp-staining is available. The method by which the inspections are made and the observations recorded can be modelled on that described in Chapter 9, though naturally they will be less detailed.

These inspections will usually be the first activity to be recorded on the maintenance chart, which will cover at least a five-year cycle so that the recurrance of all major items of work is visible.

The second activity to be recorded will be a period in each year directly after each inspection, during which the time available for maintenance is devoted to correction of minor faults observed.

The severity of exposure and the usage of the building, as well as the subjective judgement of the owner, will determine the period for redecoration work (assuming that any areas seen to be particularly defective in this respect would be specially dealt with during the remedial period referred to above). It might be reasonable to repaint externally every five years, while expecting internal decorations to have a life of seven years. On the other hand, considerations of appearance rather than protection might persuade an owner that all decorations should be renewed at five-yearly intervals. The work can, of course, be done in stages, and there is no need for the whole of the external work to be done at one time, though if contractors are employed a favourable price may be obtained for the larger contract.

Assuming that work is to be spread throughout the spring, summer and autumn period, and that the owner's own maintenance staff will be used, and in the knowledge of the number of people available, a period can be set aside in each year (perhaps in the spring) for partial external redecoration, while a similar period in the autumn is devoted to internal painting.

Other items will come up at longer intervals. While roofs should be carefully inspected each year, major overhaul will only be needed about once in twenty years. The same may be true of boundary fences and paths: a period can be allocated to partial renewal of paths and fences in years five and fifteen.

Work to the services can be similarly spread. The end-result should be that the owner can allocate a fixed sum and a fixed number of staff for maintenance work throughout the life of the building, and be prepared for all the likely contingencies.

The level of maintenance required may be difficult to ascertain. As discussed earlier, a basic decision for the owner balances the initial outlay against the amount available to be spent on maintenance year by year. If his decision has been to limit the level of maintenance to what is absolutely essential, he should be fully apprised of those areas (such as the painting of steelwork and the penetration of damp) where neglect will lead to severe deterioration, as opposed to other topics where some scruffiness may be acceptable since no structural damage is to be anticipated. Equally, the Client who wishes his prestige office to be immaculate at all times should understand that his expenditure should really be allocated to his public relations account!

Some owners will prefer to employ outside contractors for major maintenance work. This may make programming (particularly if work has to be completed during a restricted period) simpler, though it will not necessarily be cheaper – that is something that needs to be worked out for each individual case.

The owner or occupier who does not intend to carry out maintenance work with his own staff may value advice on finding suitable firms to carry out the work for him, and the best way to obtain an acceptable price. He should certainly be told which jobs should always be the subject of expert advice, and for which (see Chs. 10, 11 and 12) emergency attention is required.

Chapter 8

The economics of building

All modern business operations depend upon a reliable and continuous supply of money if they are to continue. Premises have to be provided, maintained, heated and lit; equipment, transport and staff amenities are essential: materials have to be purchased and stored.

It is rare for the goods or services produced by a business to be paid for directly they are provided: on the other hand the overheads in the form of salaries, insurances and so on produce bills which have inexorably to be met. In addition, principals expect a return upon their investment of time, money and effort.

In most cases, the finance comes at least initially from a backer such as a bank, which lends money at interest in the expectation that it will eventually be recovered and against the security of the skill and probity of the directors and a full order book. To the bank, money loaned in this way is working, whereas money simply kept on deposit is idle, so the bank seeks to loan as much money as possible at the best rates of interest it can get. Such rates may depend on market forces, or be constrained by Bank of England rates.

Compound interest

If you were to invest £100 in a savings account at 10 per cent per annum interest, after a year you would be entitled to an additional £10. You could elect to withdraw that sum when it was paid: in that case you would continue to receive £10 in each subsequent year, and the amount invested would remain constant. This is simple interest.

If, on the other hand, you elected to leave the interest accrued in the account, at the end of the first year the money in the account would be £110, so the interest paid at the end of that year would be £11. The amount in the account would then be £121. The capital would continue to grow at this accelerating rate: this is compound interest.

Provided that the interest payable is known, the amount available after any period of years can be calculated.

If the time in years is called 'x' the amount originally invested is called P (for principal) and C is the capital available for withdrawal at any time, then

$$C = P \left(\frac{1 + \text{interest rate } y}{100}\right)^x$$

so that in the example quoted, the total amount available after twelve years would be

$$C = 100 \left(\frac{1 + 10}{100}\right)^{12} = £314.$$

It can, in fact, also be useful to know how soon the capital will have doubled at a given rate of interest. This can be calculated approximately from the formula $\dfrac{70}{\% \text{ growth rates}}$ for rates up to about

10 per cent. The doubling time at 10 per cent would be approximately seven years. (See Table 8.1.)

Table 8.1 Compound interest

	Years	y = 6%	8%	10%	12%	14%	
x =	1	106	108	110	112	114	
	2	112	117	121	125	130	
	3	119	126	133	140	148	approx.
	4	126	136	146	157	169	doubling
	5	134	147	161	176	193	time
	6	142	159	177	197	219	
	7	150	171	195	221	250	
	8	159	185	214	248	285	
	9	169	200	236	277	325	
	10	179	216	259	311	371	
	11	190	233	285	348	423	
	12	201	252	314	390	482	

Capital available after x years, from a principal of £100 invested at y % per annum.

$$C = \frac{P (1 + y)^x}{100}$$

Such growth is 'exponential' and if plotted as a graph on ordinary graph paper will be shown as an accelerating curve. If it is plotted on 'log/linear' paper, it appears as a straight line – so if a known growth rate is plotted on log/linear paper it can immediately be seen whether the growth rate is actually exponential.
(See Figs. 8.1 and 8.2.)

You would notice a parallel phenomenon if you were to borrow money. If you chose to pay-off only the interest each year, you would go on paying indefinitely and the debt would never be reduced. Alterations in interest rates on mortgages in recent years (in cases where borrowers exercised an option included in their deeds, to pay a constant amount each month, irrespective of interest rates, the total repayment period being altered instead) could in some cases have meant that borrowers were paying-off **less** than the interest, and their debt was actually increasing.

If, on the other hand, you were to elect to pay-off the whole of the interest each year, plus 10 per cent of the outstanding capital (and the amount borrowed was £100 at 10 per cent per annum) you would pay £20 in the first year, £18 in the second, and ever-reducing amounts thereafter. These amounts would never actually reach zero unless at some point you chose to settle the debt with a once-for-all payment.

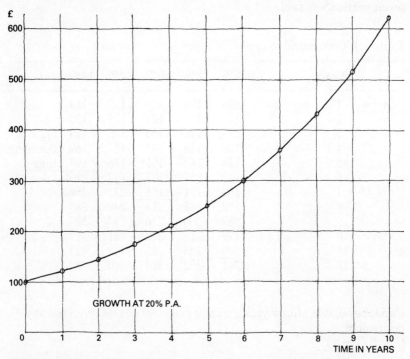

Fig. 8.1 Exponential growth

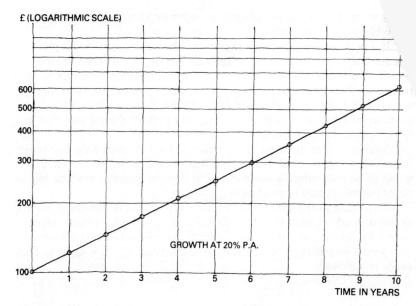

Fig. 8.2 Exponential growth shows as a straight line on log/linear paper

Because money in a savings account actually grows by the amount of the interest paid upon it, while a debt grows because of the interest the debtor has to pay, the value of a sum of money at the present and in the future is not the same. It is to one's advantage to delay the payment of bills until the latest possible date (meanwhile collecting interest on the money) while it is to the advantage of the organisations sending out the accounts to collect payment as soon as possible.

This advantage can be quantified, providing certain assumptions about prevailing interest rates and the consequent 'doubling time' are made. Inflation, which is taken to affect all financial operations equally for this purpose, is disregarded. Selecting the most suitable notional interest rate (the 'test discount rate') is crucial to the calculations, however.

Because maintaining a steady flow of cash is vital to an entrepreneur such as a builder, such calculations are basic to the success of his company. It will also be clear that a builder is able to provide a more advantageous tender if he knows that regular stage-payments will reduce his need to borrow in order to finance his overheads.

Discounted cash flow
The technique of 'discounted cash flow' allows one to calculate the present value of a future purchase on the basis of the amount that

at the present in order to have the purchase price
is needed.

tive purchaser knows that he will need to buy a piece
, whose present value is £1 000, in 5 years time, he may
et aside the money for that purpose at once. The capital he
will earn interest in the interim, and he need not, therefore,
de so much as £1 000. Providing he can make a reasonable
nate of interest rates over the five-year period, the amount that has
o be reserved can be calculated.

Similarly, if he is owed £100, which will not be paid until five years
hence, that sum is worth less to him than its face value (if he is not
going to be paid interest meanwhile). It is good business practice to
defer payments and recover debts.

The value to the business of future expenditure or future payments
at the time of calculation is the 'discounted' value. The formula given
above for arriving at money available from an initial investment at
compound interest can be rearranged to calculate P if C is known. This
reads as follows:

$$P = \frac{C}{\left(1 + \dfrac{y}{100}\right)^x}$$

In order to have £1 000 available in five years time, at an
anticipated interest rate of 10 per cent (the test discount rate) it will
thus be necessary to invest

$$\frac{1\ 000}{\left(1 + \dfrac{10}{100}\right)^5}$$

or about £621.

Selection of the most appropriate test discount rate for discounted
cash flow calculations is critical. Predictions are not invalidated by
changes in the rate of inflation, but can be seriously thrown out by a
change in the cost of borrowing money.

If the above calculation had assumed a test discount rate of 6 per
cent, the answer would have been £746, while if 14 per cent had been
taken it would have been £518. (See Table 8.2.)

These formulae, suitably rearranged, can also be used to establish
time ('I have £100 which I can invest at 6 per cent. How long before I
can afford a piece of equipment worth £140?') or interest rate ('I have
£100 to invest and wish to draw out my capital after five years to buy a
piece of equipment worth £140. What rate of interest must I obtain?')

Beware, incidentally, of part-years. An annual rate of interest may
well be paid in one lump at the end of the year.

On the other hand, if interest is paid monthly and compounded,
the return will be more than you might expect. One per cent per
month compounded will increase capital of £100 by £12.68, whereas
annual interest at 12 per cent will increase it only by £12.

Table 8.2 Discounted value

	Years	y = 6%	8%	10%	12%	14%
x =	1	94.3	92.6	90.9	89.3	87.7
	2	89.3	85.5	82.6	80.3	76.9
	3	84.0	79.4	75.2	71.4	67.6
	4	79.4	73.5	68.5	63.7	59.2
	5	74.6	68.0	62.1	56.8	51.8
	6	70.4	62.9	56.5	50.8	45.7
	7	66.7	58.5	51.3	45.2	40.0
	8	62.9	54.1	46.7	40.3	35.1
	9	59.2	50.3	42.4	36.1	30.8
	10	55.9	46.3	38.6	32.2	27.0
	11	52.9	42.9	35.1	28.8	23.6
	12	49.8	39.7	31.8	25.6	20.7

Principal which must be invested to produce available capital of £100 after a period of x years invested at y %

$$P = \frac{c}{\left(1 + \frac{y}{100}\right)^x}$$

Money supply

The rate of growth of the economy very much depends upon the amount of money available for business ventures, and the effect of a shortage of money for investment, and therefore high interest rates can be particularly critical for the building industry.

Without launching into an evaluation of the economic strategies adopted by successive governments in the effort to contain inflation, it must be noted that control of the amount of 'new' money in circulation – that is, money 'printed' rather than reflecting value for goods or services provided – by altering the base lending rate are common. This distorts the effect of market pressures and may have unanticipated effects on the viability of businesses.

Whether or not such methods are efficient in effecting their major aim, they have an immediate significance for any business in which cash flow is critical.

All businesses need to predict their future cash needs and arrange to have cash available to finance them. They need to obtain that money as cheaply as possible.

The Architect's office

The Architect is paid through fees, which become due only after services have been provided. The continuing efficiency of his practice depends on a flow of fees from completed work – but many months of work may be needed before any fees at all are paid, at the outset.

The Architect has usually, therefore, had to obtain capital from some outside source in order to fit out his office with even the most basic equipment and survive during the early, lean years while he was building-up his reputation. A first charge on his income for a considerable period after he has become established is likely to be interest payments and part repayment of the principal of such early finance. He will probably have predicted the date at which he hopes to retire and arranged to spread these payments right up to that time, so as to minimise the burden.

This capital will, among other things, have provided suitable furniture, decorations and equipment, which do not, therefore, have to be allowed for elsewhere in his calculations, though he will allow something for periodic refurbishment.

The next large charge against income will be the rent and rates on the office premises. The practice cannot survive without adequate space, because cramped assistants would find it impossible to work effectively. Offices in an expensive area are less likely to be considered essential, providing they are accessible and reasonably visible: his office and its notice board are one of the few forms of advertisement that the Architect is allowed.

These premises then need to be heated and lit, and provided with a telephone service. There is little leeway for deferring payment of such accounts.

Stationery, printing and postage take a sizeable slice from running expenses. The quality of letterheads and the clarity of printing are important not only in establishing the 'image' of the practice, but also in actual efficiency.

Transport for easy site access, in the form of office cars or railway warrants can also be a considerable expense.

Salaries for professional and technical staff are clearly a major and important expense, on which no Architect who valued the expertise and loyalty of his staff would skimp. Clerical support is also vital: technical staff should not have to spend time fending off unwanted visitors, answering telephones or filing when they could be solving technical problems.

There are also insurances, not only of the premises and to cover the safety and well-being of staff, but also against claims for professional negligence, to be allowed for. The professional responsibility of the Architect seems continually to be extended by the Courts, and he would be unfair to his clients if he did not ensure that their reasonable claims against him (and his assistants) could not be met in full.

Taxes, too, must be paid.

111

Finally, of course, the Architect expects that his professional training and experience will be adequately rewarded, and that when all his expenses have been met he will himself be able to support a reasonable standard of living.

It can, therefore, be seen that it is essential to ensure that time and the other resources of the office are used efficiently. This does not mean, of course, that any problem will receive less than the attention necessary. It does mean that everyone must be aware that time must be budgeted responsibly, so that the best use is made of the resources available for each job.

It is possible to predict with some accuracy at an early stage in any job what the fees it will attract will amount to. It is also possible to cost out all the overheads listed above, and so to arrive at a cost per man-hour which includes all of these including the assistant's own salary – a figure that may easily amout to two-and-a-half to three times the hourly salary. From these figures the number of man-hours which can reasonably be allocated to the project can be worked out. These hours must then be budgeted – so many at briefing stage, so many for sketch design (possibly the most flexible category) so many for production drawings, for site supervision, for record drawings and feedback, and so on. (See Fig. 8.3.)

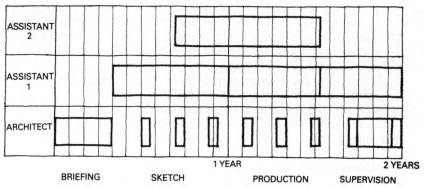

Fig. 8.3 It is important to know how time is spent

Naturally the situation will never be allowed to occur when the Architect refuses to spend any more time on a particular aspect of a job because the time allowance is overspent. None the less it is vital, if he is to run an efficient office that everyone should be aware of time being spent, and ready to spend the time available in productive and useful ways.

The offices of the Consulting Engineers, Quantity Surveyor, and other professionals in the design team will be subject to similar constraints. Although all of these exist to provide a service they can only do so if their accounts are in a healthy state at the year's end.

The Client

Not all clients are actively seeking a maximum cash return for the money they invest in buildings, but virtually all are interested in obtaining value for money. It is possible to divide client organisations into three main groups as follows.

Clients who need buildings

A building may be necessary to a client in order that he can carry on his business, whether that is a money-making concern, like a factory or shop, or a service such as a hospital or school. In either case the cost of adapting existing premises, renting a building put up by someone else, and sometimes of continuing to operate from existing, cramped accommodation, is likely to be compared with the cost of new provision. The advantages of modern, tailor-made facilities will be evaluated, as well as the residual value when the building is no longer needed. Clients in this category usually have to raise the necessary capital.

Clients who wish for new buildings

Some clients, who happen to have money available, or have an available source of cheap money, may seek improved conditions which are not strictly necessary, since they feel these are worth paying for. A family may spend an inheritance, or the proceeds of a promotion, on a new and better house, or a firm may wish for headquarters which it feels better reflect its prestige. This client is looking for quality, but is still looking for value for money.

To either of the clients referred to above, cost in use will be significant. There is a need to relate capital provision with maintenance and running costs, through the techniques of terotechnology and discounted cost flow techniques will be used in determining the optimum level of present expenditure.

The Client with money to invest

The third group of clients includes those who see building as a worthwhile investment for their money.

Such a client will be very well aware of the rents that the market will bear, for particular classes of accommodation, and expects that the building he buys will reflect this understanding of business realities. He knows that even an empty building may appreciate in capital value – at some states of the market at a higher rate than his capital could be expected to appreciate if invested elsewhere.

This category includes not only the speculative developer of houses or office blocks, but also the hotelier who lets out rooms with service. Each will provide a precise specification of requirements based on detailed study and experience of their market, and this must be respected by the designer. An apparently small deviation may drop the lettable accommodation into a lower price-bracket, while calculations of the return on the investment can be invalidated by a failure to accept cash limits.

The builder's business

The builder, like the Architect, has overheads. He needs premises – though he is likely to be less interested in promoting his image than in acquiring a site with ample space for storage of materials and plant, room for workshops, and the possibility of future expansion. He will be pleased to take an opportunity of proving his reputation for quality by putting-up a sound building for himself – provided he can see that this is a good investment.

The builder must, above all, be a sound businessman, for cash flow is vital to his success. The usual pattern of a contract is that very large sums have to be paid for materials and labour which are needed to carry out work, whilst the work will not be paid for until it is complete – and then, even, only subject to a sizeable retention. Clearly, even though he exercises the best business methods, paying at the latest possible date while pressing for the earliest possible remittances from his debtors, the gap between paying and being paid will never disappear completely. The sum he expects to be paid eventually is of course larger than his debts, but it takes a sound application of discounted cash flow techniques to establish the continued financial viability of the firm.

In addition, the builder must finance unsuccessful tendering, and will wish to retain the services of his management staff and top craftsmen through the lean periods when contracts are sparse. He may see the advantage of indulging in speculative work, which demands an even higher level of capitalisation, while promising enhanced returns.

Should such a builder lose the confidence of his bank, he is at once unable to continue in business: cash flow is vital to him. He can rarely expect to finance one job on the profits of the previous one, and is likely in any case to wish to reinvest any unusual profit by improving his premises and plant to his future advantage.

It is little to be wondered at that the attractiveness or otherwise of a project to a builder often comes down to little more than the rate and regularity with which he can expect to be paid. He will be readier to tender for work for an organisation known to certify fairly and pay promptly than for one with a weaker reputation in this respect – and will put in keener prices as a result.

Contracts

Contracts are designed to be fair to both the client and the builder.

The former should not be expected to pay for value he has yet to receive, while the latter should not remain unpaid for completed work. The Joint Contracts Tribunal contracts in general use are well tested and understood from this point of view, and work well for new buildings and substantial alterations and extensions, where the work to be undertaken can be seen with some accuracy from the outset.

It is in the case of renovations and smaller alterations, where the extent of the work to be done can only be seen after operations have started that some difficulty is liable to arise. Both builder and building owner need to have a sound idea of the scope of the finance involved, so as to arrange their affairs to the best advantage, yet this information may simply not be available.

Three main types of contract are in use to deal with this difficulty (though there have been experiments with some variations).

One is the type of contract under which work is measured provisionally, so as to provide a schedule of rates against which the whole of the work actually carried out will be remeasured and costed. This assures the builder of being paid for all that he undertakes at rates he considers adequate (and which are monitored by an independent Quantity Surveyor) but leaves the owner with little advance idea of the total expenditure he can expect to incur. He can be happy, however, that the rates are not exorbitant, and that he will be asked to pay only for work actually required.

The second type is a lump-sum contract against a specification only, in which a builder is asked to undertake all the work that may be necessary (with a minimum of restrictions to omit particular possible but unlikely items) for a global sum that will not be varied. Both parties know how much money is to change hands, so they may see advantages in this arrangement, but since the builder will be anxious to cover his costs, he may include for all manner of work that is unlikely to be needed, and the price is liable to be high, so the arrangement is difficult to recommend.

The third option is for a 'prime cost' contract, under which the builder will be paid the actual cost to him of labour, materials and so on, plus a fee for management and profit (preferably not calculated as a percentage). The incentive on the builder to minimise costs is lost.

It will be seen that the position in the contract of the Quantity Surveyor is crucial in such cases. Mutual trust can be greatly enhanced if the whole operation is under the watchful eye of an experienced and trusted Quantity Surveyor.

Terotechnology

The idea of terotechnology, which was first applied to the provision of industrial plant, but has a much wider potential use, is to make people realise that capital and revenue expenditure are both 'money'. These sums tend to be regarded as though they were as different as apples and blackberries, and the notion that extra capital expenditure might save future revenue is apparently hard for some building owners to grasp. Often this is because the two 'kinds' of money come, in fact, from different sources: the capital to build a house may be borrowed from a building society, while the cost of insurances and repainting is covered from the salary cheque; the government may lend the money to fund a new school, while the rates bear the brunt of the running cost. Following this line, it can be forgotten that the salary has to cover the mortgage repayments, and the rates have to pay back loans (with interest) to central government, too.

If true life-cycle costs, taking into account the discounted value of every expenditure that will be incurred because the building exists, are made, a true idea of the most economical and sensible way to lay out money can be obtained. Such a calculation needs to start from a careful appreciation of the length of life of the building, after which it will be considered so obsolete as to need to be replaced or to be substantially upgraded. It should then be assumed that the capital cost will be paid off over the whole of this period, and allowances for the amount of money to be set aside for running and maintenance costs as well as repairs and replacements over that period can be made. Against this sum can be set the residual cost of the building – for sale or as the basis for alterations – at the end of that period. Such calculations make possible a sound comparison between alternative suggested forms of building and levels of specification. (See Fig. 8.4.)

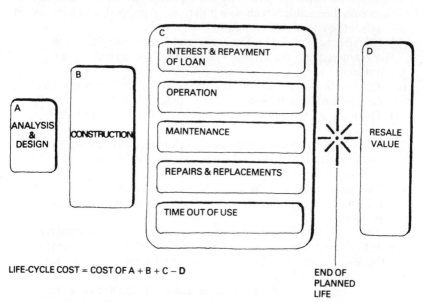

C

INTEREST & REPAYMENT OF LOAN

OPERATION

B

A

ANALYSIS & DESIGN

CONSTRUCTION

MAINTENANCE

D

RESALE VALUE

REPAIRS & REPLACEMENTS

TIME OUT OF USE

LIFE-CYCLE COST = COST OF A + B + C – D

END OF PLANNED LIFE

Fig. 8.4 Terotechnology is concerned with life-cycle costs

Chapter 9

Building surveys

The objects of preparing a building survey may not always be the same. They are, however, likely to include the recording of accurate data regarding:

(a) Accommodation provided by the building, the number and size of rooms, the facilities with which they are equipped, and the ways in which the rooms are related to each another.

(b) The structure of the building, the materials from which it is constructed and the methods of construction, as well as the finishes.

(c) The condition of both the structure and the finishes, with sufficient data to provide a basis for the later diagnosis of faults.

(d) The nature and runs of all the service installations, and their condition.

(e) The site of the building, including information regarding the boundaries, driveways and paths, major planting, general levels and the positions, depths, and condition of drains.

(f) The surroundings of the site, roads, services available, and general information regarding the nature, use and condition of adjoining properties.

There should be sufficient detail to facilitate the preparation of accurate drawings as a basis for alteration or extension schemes, and for the initial diagnosis of faults so that the desirability of any further tests can be established.

In order for these purposes to be achieved with the greatest possible efficiency it is essential that a systematic method of observation and record should be adopted. The person making the inspection needs to be properly equipped and there is no doubt that the result will generally be most satisfactory if it is undertaken by a team of two. This is not simply because measurements are most easily taken if there is someone to hold each end of the tape, but also because it works well to have one person to read-off information while another records it. It is also helpful to have the cross-check of a second pair of eyes. Although one of the pair will usually be responsible for the end-result, the other needs some specialist knowledge, and shouldn't just be the tea boy taken along for the ride. (See Fig. 9.1.)

Fig. 9.1 First impressions on site

Equipment

The equipment required will include the following.
(a) Clipboard and an adequate supply of paper. Many people use squared paper, but this is largely a matter of personal preference. A4 is the most easily-handled size. Enough paper will be needed for a separate sheet to be devoted to each room as well as to each floor, one to each elevation, and one to the site and surroundings.
(b) Felt-tip or fibre-tip pens in a variety of colours. The sketches will be less confusing if different colours are used for structure, drains, water services, electrical installation and so on.

(c) A tape and a rigid ruler for taking measurements.

(d) A torch, to illuminate crevices, cavities and the spaces in lofts and below suspended ground-floors.

(e) Binoculars, which may make it possible to inspect roofs and chimneys without scaling them.

(f) A crowbar or other similar tool to facilitate the removal of inspection-chamber covers.

(g) Potassium permanganate crystals or other harmless colouring material to assist the tracing of drains.

(h) Ladders and steps, which may be made available by the building owner. The inspector should never climb a ladder unless the bottom is firmly wedged and his assistant remains at the lower level.

(i) A camera, which may provide a rapid means of recording detail in a permanent form, but cannot substitute for annotated and dimensioned notes.

Method

Interior

The inspection should begin with an overall tour of the property to gain a general impression of the arrangement of the accommodation and the relationships between the rooms.

This will be easiest if an attempt is made at the same time to identify the major structural features of the building so that the underlying logic of the building can be understood. It may be that an original structure with later alterations or extensions can be seen, or that it becomes clear that the use of certain standardised components has been an important controlling feature of the final layout. The object of the initial tour is to obtain a grasp of the major features of the building, against which detail can be understood.

It should then be possible to draw generally proportionate plans of each floor, identifying the various rooms, which can provide a basis for the more detailed inspection. Figure 9.2 shows an example.

Each space in turn should next be visited for a rigorous inspection and record, and as each is completed the fact should be noted on the relevant floor-plan. This gives a good indication of progress as well as ensuring that no space is overlooked.

In each room a floor-plan and internal elevations should be drawn, to show the materials which are visible and their condition as well as any detail regarding underlying structures that can be inferred. Such detail as windows and doors, with their frames, pipework, radiators and electricity points, skirtings, cornices, built-in fittings, and appliances must be included. Cupboards must be opened and their interiors included in the inspection and record. If it is possible to infer the purpose of pipework this should be noted, though tracing services

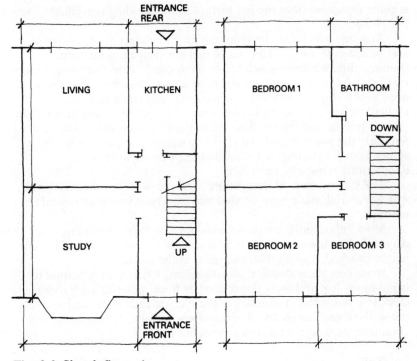

Fig. 9.2 Sketch floor-plan

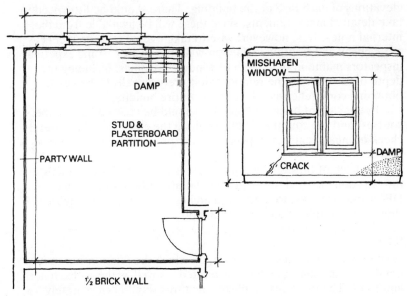

Fig. 9.3 More detailed notes

is generally easier once the full picture of the building is available. (See Fig. 9.3.)

Any sign which may be symptomatic of a defect must, of course, also be carefully noted. This would include visible cracking and staining, dirt, windows which fail to open easily, defective plaster and rusty metal as well as obvious decay or missing features. There is no need at this stage to attempt diagnosis, but any crack should be meticulously observed, and notes made of its position, length, width at various points, and the relationship of the planes on either side of it. Similarly the position and extent of any sign of dampness, whether it shows as paper peeling of a wall, dullness of paintwork or discolouration must be recorded.

The general state of decorations, and the skill (or otherwise) with which materials have been applied may also be relevant and should be noted.

Most importantly, measurements must be taken, including diagonals (for few rooms are truly rectangular) and these must include height checked at more than one point in the room.

In making these detailed investigations, it is generally helpful to begin in the loft and work down floor by floor, entering each room in clockwise sequence, starting from the stair on each floor, and studying the walls of each room also in clockwise sequence. This helps to eliminate the danger of missing any space out.

Exterior

The external inspection starts with the sketching of proportionate elevations of each face of the building. There should be little need to take detailed measurements, since these will be available from the internal notes. It is, however, wise to take overall measurements as a cross-check and to provide data on wall thicknesses. Some experienced inspectors maintain that detail of window openings, including the depth of reveals and the relationship to return walls is the key to obtaining comprehensive data on the entire building.

In the case of brickwork heights should be recorded as numbers of courses, and the counting of bricks along the course can be a useful check of measurements, especially if the presence of any cut bricks is noted.

On each of these elevations, features must be plotted exactly as this was done in the interior. Particular attention should be paid to DPCs and airbricks, to lintols and arches and to the roof. Figure 9.4 shows an example of an elevational note.

Site

A site plan should finally be made, on which the relationship of the building to the site boundaries is plotted, as well as the paths, fences and trees. The positions of all such features should be accurately

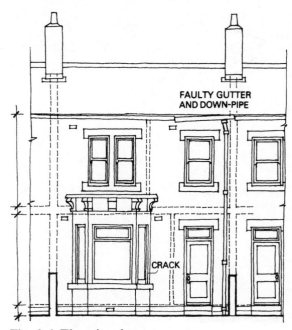

FAULTY GUTTER
AND DOWN-PIPE

CRACK

Fig. 9.4 Elevational notes

plotted by triangulation if there is any question of alteration or extension to the premises.

It is also essential to raise the covers of inspection chambers, not only to inspect the condition of the drains but also so that a correct drainage plan can be sketched. If there is ambiguity, as is often the case, as to which branch serves which appliance, the use of staining crystals to identify the outflow from any connection is helpful.

If the entry positions of the water, gas, electricity and telephone services into the building have been plotted it should be a straightforward matter to determine and indicate upon the site plan the course of those services across the site.

It is also extremely important to make fairly detailed notes of the buildings or land surrounding the site. There are two reasons for this. Firstly, the information may be very relevant to the future use which can sensibly be made of the premises being inspected, and secondly it has sometimes occurred that damage to adjoining property has been attributed by the owners to building operations next door. If there is a record to prove whether or not damage existed before any such operations began this can be helpful is resolving subsequent disputes. Figure 9.5 shows a typical site plan.

Photographs
Photographs provide a useful record of existing conditions and can

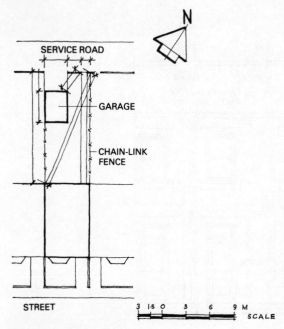

Fig. 9.5 Notes on the site

usefully enrich the material collected. They cannot take the place of detailed measurements and notes, but can appropriately be the means by which attention is drawn to particular points. They are especially useful as illustrations to the eventual written report.

Record drawings

On the basis of the site notes, plan sections and elevations of the building and its environment can be prepared. Where nothing more than a record of the condition of a building is needed, proportionate freehand sketches may be suitable. If, however, there is any question of future alterations or extensions accurate drawings should be made.

These drawings should indicate the position of every feature which has been noted, and give cross-references to the descriptive notes included in the written report. If there is important cracking, it is usually helpful to include separate small-scale drawings on which those cracks are shown in an exaggerated form. This provides a useful basis for diagnosis. Figure 9.6 shows this.

The scale appropriate for the drawings will, of course, vary with the subject, but it is important that there should be drawings to a scale small enough to allow the complex to be understood as a whole. This may necessitate the preparation of separate drawings to show detail of observed features.

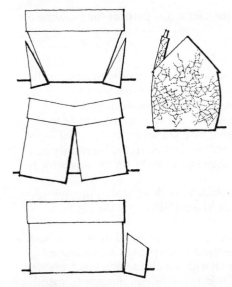

Fig. 9.6 Showing cracks

Written reports

The report should begin with a general description of the siting, structure and purpose of the building. A more detailed description of the materials and method of construction should follow, after which attention is drawn to the particular features noted during the inspection. The material may be illustrated by photographs, and should include unambiguous cross-references to the detailed drawings.

The features described should be classified by type rather than by location, so that 'Windows', 'Chimneys' or 'Damp' might be among the chosen headings, rather than 'First Floor' or 'Kitchen'.

This part of the description should be purely factual and concentrate on a precise description of what has been observed.

The next section of the report should make tentative diagnoses of the possible causes of observed defects, with evidence and explanations where these are relevant and helpful, and including suggestions for further tests or investigation. This could include a recommendation to consult a specialist, whether that was a research organisation, an academic institution or a specialist firm.

Finally, general information about the state of the building in relation to its age and type, recommendations about the work needed to put it into good order, and its suitability for the contemplated purpose should be given.

The whole report should be technical in tone, and should avoid the use of the special language adopted by estate agents.

Attention must be drawn to the fact if any parts of the building or its structure proved inaccessible.

Periodic reports

Owners such as the Church authorities often require regular periodic reports upon their properties. Once a comprehensive report on such a property has been prepared, subsequent inspections should be comparatively straightforward to make, and the reports simple to prepare, since the work is facilitated by comparison with earlier inspections. Such surveys must none the less be treated seriously and carried out conscientiously since the responsibility on the inspector is not lessened.

It is useful and common to include in such a report a memoir of points to which particular attention should be paid at the next inspection.

Reports on properties not changing hands should draw the owner's attention to the likely effects of neglect to carry out recommended deeper inspections and work, which will usually include much greater expenditure at some later date. Owners are often reluctant to spend money on putting right what appear to be minor defects, and it may be helpful to make drawings to indicate the consequences to the structure, and in future expenditure, of failure to do so.

Chapter 10

Cracks

All buildings are subjected, both during construction and throughout their lifetimes, to continual slight movement. This may be due to expansion and contraction as the temperatures change or as materials dry out, or decay. Superimposed loads such as furniture or moving occupants, wind or snow and slight earth movements may also have this effect. Such movements have to be allowed for in the original design.

Because many building materials, and particularly those employed as finishes, are relatively inelastic, and it may be expensive to detail to allow for every anticipated movement, some cracking may be inevitable, especially during the first year of a building's life. The building generally settles after that period, when such superficial cracking can be made good in reasonable confidence that it will not recur.

Other and more severe damage may be due to loads not anticipated when the building was designed or to loss of strength because of the deterioration of materials, or to more serious earth movement.

All cracks should be critically examined so that the cause can be identified and dealt with before any attempt is made to make the damage good. The correct diagnosis may require careful observation over a period of some months, during which time temporary shoring may be necessary.

Any structure where the centre of gravity falls outside the middle third of the base is generally considered to be inherently unsafe. This has to be taken into account in evaluating the stability of any wall which is leaning or bulging.

No crack should ever be thought of in isolation. The parts of a building must be thought of as interrelated components of a whole, and the first step in diagnosis is to study the way in which all the loads are transferred.

Not all cracks render a building unstable, but they are likely to have an effect on the watertightness of the building, which might lead to consequential damage. Even those cracks not regarded as potentially dangerous should, therefore, receive attention.

Principal causes of cracks

Earth movements

Foundations may fail for a variety of reasons. All buildings settle, and foundations are designed to spread the total load in such a way that the settlement is equalised across the entire building. It is in cases where uneven, or 'differential' settlement occurs that cracking may be caused.

Supposing that the foundations were adequately designed at the outset, and correctly constructed, failure implies that the bearing capacity of the ground below has been reduced for some reason. This might be due to one of the following factors:

Loss of lateral support

If building works take place on an adjoining site, the effect may be to allow lateral movement of the ground beneath foundations even where the excavation is beyond the 45° angle within which the load is assumed to be spread. Figure 10.1 indicates how this could occur. The right to support from an adjoining site is clearly established in the common law, and if loss of such support is suspected as the cause of damage, a solicitor should be consulted.

Change in subterranean watercourse

Earthmoving operations at some distance from a building can be responsible for changes in the courses of underground rivers, which may be diverted so as to endanger foundations by erosion. Leaking drains, or soakaways too close to buildings can have a similar effect, which is particularly marked in chalky soils.

Mining subsidence

The action of coal-mining beneath a site causes a heaving of the surface followed by a drop, the effect being much as though a wave passed across the surface. The effect is largely predictable, and happens once-and-for-all.

The damage done to buildings not specifically designed to withstand such conditions can be severe, but compensation is available

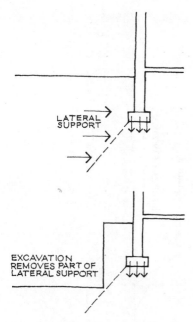

Fig. 10.1 Footings may slip due to loss of lateral support

from the National Coal Board where such damage is demonstrably due to their operations. Figure 10.2 shows diagrammatically the movement involved.

The National Coal Board provides very helpful advice on the design of buildings for mining areas, which should be followed in every respect. The precautions which may be recommended are likely to include providing heavy piers between openings of limited size, 'compartmenting' the building, and increasing the falls allowed on gutters and drains. (See Fig. 10.3.)

Consolidation of the soil

Building on made ground demands great care in the design of foundations if differential settlement is to be avoided. It is not always appreciated that on many ordinary sites there are pockets of fill (where field ditches once existed, or wells have been filled, for example) where the ground can be similarly expected to become consolidated over a period of years. This can result in an ordinary strip foundation being expected to span a void, and is therefore a potential source of foundation failure.

Shrinkable clay

Many clay soils contract when dry and expand when they are again wetted, and the process can continue indefinitely. The cracks which may be caused in buildings subjected to the movement involved have

128

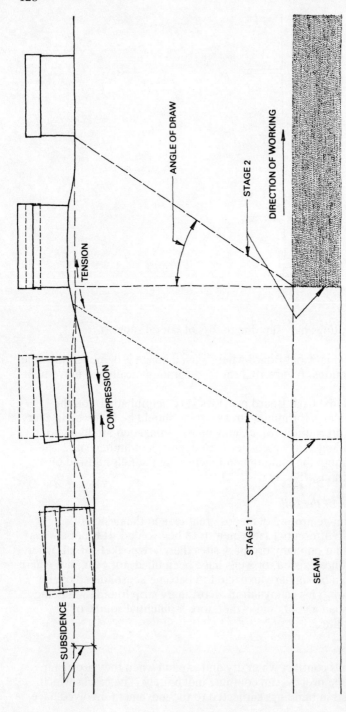

Fig. 10.2 Movement due to mining

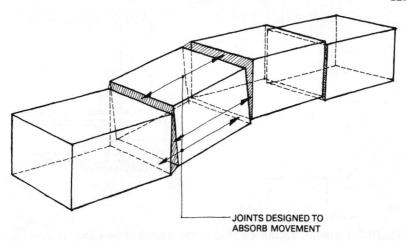

Fig. 10.3 The NCB advises on the construction of buildings in mining
areas

much in common with those caused by mining subsidence, excepting
that they are liable to recur, and may open and close seasonally.

The effect is exacerbated by the proximity of trees, especially
those which have been felled without the removal of the roots, and
where these are present continual swelling may be encountered over a
period of some years. Such roots can be destroyed by the injection of
sodium chlorate. Figure 10.4 shows the effect of such roots
diagrammatically.

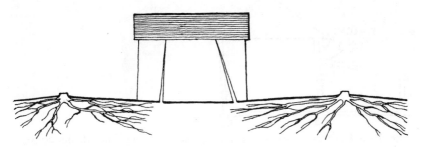

Fig. 10.4 The danger of tree roots in shrinkable clay

Frost

Expansion of water in the ground beneath buildings when it freezes
causing 'frost heave', can be sufficient to raise pavings, and in extreme
conditions to damage shallow foundations as well as site concrete in
unoccupied buildings. Frost may also, by breaking-up the earth below
shallow foundations, reduce its bearing pressure, causing potential
failure. For this reason modern foundations are either reinforced or

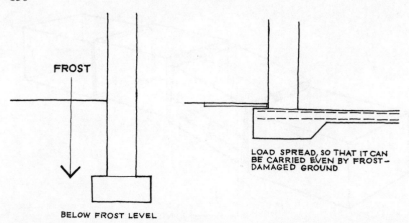

FROST

LOAD SPREAD, SO THAT IT CAN BE CARRIED EVEN BY FROST-DAMAGED GROUND

BELOW FROST LEVEL

Fig. 10.5 Foundations must go below frost level or be reinforced

taken to a level below that at which frost can be expected to occur. (See Fig. 10.5.)

Overload

A frequent cause of structural failure is the addition of extra loading to an existing structure which was not designed to support it.

For example, the roof or floor of a new extension may be carried on an existing outer wall, or a lean-to roof may be placed so as to exert a lateral thrust, as is shown in Fig. 10.6.

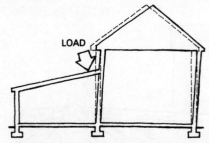

LOAD

Fig. 10.6 Lateral thrusts can cause serious damage if not designed for

The insertion of a window into a wall, or the insertion of a larger one than previously existed, may cause overloading of the abutments. Whereas the lintol inserted is usually carefully chosen for its ability to transmit the whole of the loads from above, less attention may have been paid to the bearing capacity of the remaining areas of wall. (See Fig. 10.7)

Overloads are likely to cause bulging as well as cracking, and may push a wall so far out of true as to endanger its stability. This is particularly true where loads have been asymmetrically imposed.

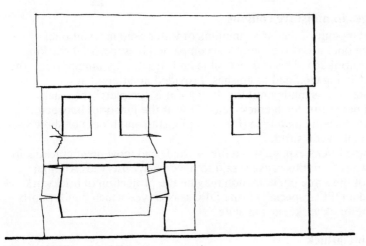

Fig. 10.7 Overload due to an opening

Temperature changes

The coefficient of expansion due to temperature change varies widely with different materials, but virtually all materials are susceptible to appreciable movement. This can have two important effects:

1. Any very long structure will be subject to cumulative movement. Expansion joints are usually incorporated into modern buildings to isolate and minimise the effect of such movement, but if the break is not complete damage can still occur.
2. Assemblies of different materials are subjected to internal stresses due to thermal movement unless they are carefully detailed to take this into account, and may fail. (See Fig. 10.8)

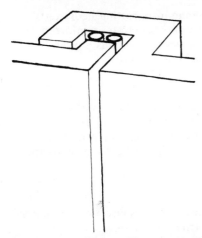

Fig. 10.8 Damage will ensue if allowance for differential thermal expansion is not made when detailing

Changes in moisture content

The drying-out of the large amounts of water used in traditional building operations is generally accompanied by superficial cracking due to shrinkage. This is irreversible and structurally unimportant, the damage being confined to finishes. Provided no attempt at reinstatement is made until the drying-out is complete, the cracks should not recur. Such cracks may show at the junctions between different backing materials (for example, stud and block) or show as crazing all over a surface.

Some bricks expand when first wetted, and movement cracking in brick walls from this cause is said to have been observed. Another effect of the same phenomenon may be the projection of brickwork beyond a DPC, especially if the DPC is of a type which bonds poorly with the brickwork, such as slate.

Sulphate attack

Cement-based mortars and those containing hydraulic lime which are subjected to lengthy saturation are liable to expand. The tricalcium aluminate they contain is attacked by soluble sulphates in soil, bricks or flue gases. Boiler flues are often damaged by this action if they are unlined. Colliery waste used in hardcore and in ground form as aggregate in 'black' mortar in industrial areas is liable to similar action. In either case the evidence may be in the form of bulging or cracking.

Unslaked quicklime

Fragments of inadequately-slaked lime are liable to 'pop' or expand in damp conditions.

Rust

Since iron oxide occupies more space than iron, rusting steel exerts pressure on surrounding structures. If water penetrates reinforced concrete through hair cracks, so that the steel rusts, this is often followed by spalling of the cover, pushed off by rust.

Decay of timber

Where timber is built into masonry and decays as the result of biological attack (see Ch. 12) the masonry may lose important support and be in danger of collapse. This may occur where a partition is carried on a beam or joist which is damaged, or where joist-ends are built into masonry.

Vibration

Buildings which are close to motorways or other sources of continuous or violent vibration may be damaged from that cause.

Poor design or construction

Walls with an excessive slenderness ratio, poor bonding (especially near quoins, where lateral restraint is required) lack of or failure of ties in cavities and the failure to spread loads properly with pads can all have an adverse effect on the building's performance.

Possibly more important is lack of care in placing loads, so that stresses are not exerted centrally, and unplanned lateral thrusts are imposed.

Where adjacent blocks are of differing construction, (as might be the case where one wing was a single-storey loadbearing brick construction, abutting a framed block, for example) the junction is very liable to show cracking unless the joint is very carefully designed, because the distribution of loads and general structural behaviour of the two parts are different. If the amount of settlement is different in the two blocks cracking is almost bound to occur.

Visible signs

The visual evidence of failure – the patterns of cracks and bulges – may be ambiguous. Certainly it is rare for the cause to be immediately evident. However,

Cracking associated with bulging may be due to:
(a) Failure of device intended to give intermediate support, such as an upper floor.
(b) Expansion or corrosion of a structure behind the wall pushing it outward.
(c) Failure or absence of cavity ties.

Cracking associated with leaning outward may be due to:
(a) Lateral thrust from roof.
(b) Foundation failure.

Diagonal cracks running upwards and outwards from window or other openings may be due to:
(a) Overload.
(b) Differential settlement.

Diagonal cracks running inwards from the corners of windows or other openings may be due to:
(a) Failure of lintol.

Overall crazing of rendering or plaster may be due to:
(a) Different rates of drying-out of materials.
(b) Differential thermal expansion.
(c) Chemical action between materials.

Vertical cracks between the corners of windows on different floors may
be due to:
(a) Poor jointing between different constructions.
(b) Shrinkage or expansion of materials.

Long diagonal cracks running from ground to roof, especially if more
than one can be seen, may be due to:
(a) Differential settlement.

Diagnosis

It is essential to establish the actual cause of cracks and bulges before
any attempt at remedial action is made, since unless the cause is
obviated the damage is likely to recur.

Diagnosis does, however, require detailed study of the entire
building and its surroundings. It is often helpful to look for signs of
similar damage to adjacent buildings, which can sometimes throw a
helpful light on the problem.

It is also usually important (though building owners are sometimes
difficult to convince of the fact) to monitor the defects over a period of
time. If thermal movement or the action of shrinkable clay is
suspected, observations over an entire season will be imperative.

Answers to five questions will help to determine the cause of
observed symptoms.
1. How long is the crack?
   It may be that the crack can be traced from ground to roof, or it
   may be more localised. Elevations should be drawn on which all the
   observed defects are clearly plotted. It is important to remember
   that cracking will follow the path of least resistance, and may pass
   almost undetectably around window frames, for example.
2. Is it wider at top or bottom?
   Micrometer readings can be taken to determine the width of the
   crack at various points, and the resulting shape can usefully be
   plotted on to the elevation in an exaggerated form, as shown in
   Fig. 10.9.
3. Which side is moving?
   From careful examination, including the use of plumb line and spirit
   level, or of a theodolite if the crack is inaccessible, it should be
   possible to establish which part of the building has remained in
   position and which has moved. This, too, should be indicated on the
   drawing.
4. Is there bulging?
   It is unusual for the movement to be solely in a flat plane. Any
   third-dimensional tilt or bulge should be found and estimated.
5. Does the crack lengthen, widen or close?

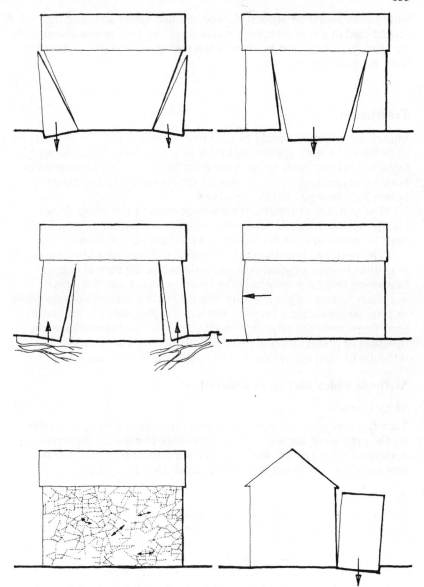

Fig. 10.9 Exaggerated sketches reveal the causes of cracks

Carefully kept records of regular observations will establish what movement, if any, is taking place.

From the answers to these questions it is possible to see just what movement has caused the defect. Consideration should make it clear what forces would be needed to produce such movement, and this should lead to a reasonable appreciation of the most probable cause of the damage, which may be established with more certainty by further tests and examination.

Treatment

Immediate attention should be paid to any crack which can be seen on both sides of a wall, appears suddenly or is very long. Such attention, however, is most likely to be in the form of shoring or examination or both – it is generally futile to attempt the correction of any defect before the cause has been determined.

The first step in treatment must be to remove the cause. Other means must be found of supporting the excess load, the rusting steel must be replaced (and the source of water sealed) and so on.

The next step is to assess the possibility of returning any misplaced structures to their original position without causing further damage. Supposing that (as is generally the case) this is not possible, it is necessary to make a comparative assessment of the merits of rebuilding or providing additional support. On this it is impossible to set useful guidelines, since the relative importance of cost and appearance, the demands of preservation of an original structure, and the physical difficulty of carrying out the work are all likely to relevant.

Methods which may be considered

Metal tie-rods
Such ties may pass through a floor structure, supporting metal plates on the exterior of the wall, or they may seek to enhance the joint between a floor and the wall to obtain support. It is very important that such ties should not be overtightened. (See Fig. 10.10.)

Buttressing
If there is space available and the appearance is not objected to, it may be simpler and more positive to arrange buttresses or piers than to insert ties. It is essential that there should be a proper bond between the old and new masonry. (See Fig. 10.11.)

Where cavity walls are defective because of absent or corroded ties it may not be necessary to take down and rebuild the entire wall, if sections can be cut out to allow ties to be inserted.

If a spreading roof structure causes cracking by exerting a lateral thrust, the insertion of collars may relieve the pressure.

Making-good cracks
Where cracks remain, but the wall is no longer dangerous, it is necessary that they should be repaired to preserve the water-resistance

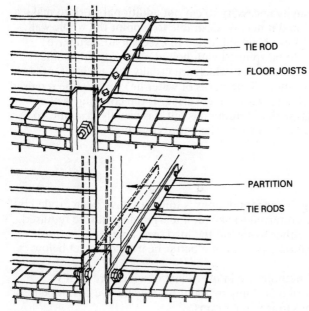

Fig. 10.10 Tie rod

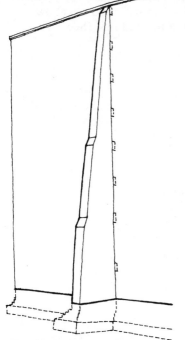

Fig. 10.11 Buttressing

of the wall. It is usually necessary to cut out additional work to make a satisfactory repair, and it may be desirable to repoint the whole wall.

Timbers which have been subjected to excess load, and have begun to split need to be splinted with bolted plates on either side.

Cracks in flat-roof finishes (which are usually due to differential thermal expansion, often where pools of water lie) can best be repaired by replacing a much larger area of covering. If the covering is of a short-lived material such as bituminous felt it is usually desirable to take the opportunity of replacing the entire covering.

Foundations

Where the bearing under foundations is found to have been eroded by one of the agencies referred to above, underpinning may be required.

This may aim either to spread the load over a wider area or to deepen the foundation in search of a better bearing or to get below frost level.

A number of methods are in use, some of which are highly specialised and carried out only by the firms which have developed them. They fall into four main groups.

1. The injection of cement/clay grout into the earth below foundations in order to stabilise the soil. Chemical grouts are also used. This method provides a measure of water-resistance, and can allow adjacent excavation below the level of the footings. (See Fig. 10.12.)

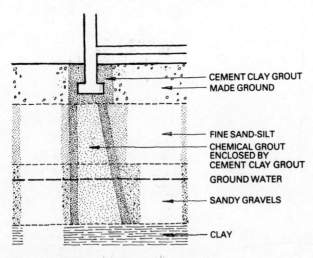

Fig. 10.12 Underpinning by injection

2. The insertion of reinforced concrete beams supported on brick or concrete piers. The wall has to be temporarily supported on timber needles or permanent stools. (See Fig. 10.13.)

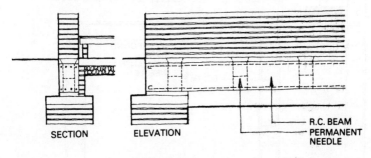

SECTION   ELEVATION

R.C. BEAM
PERMANENT NEEDLE

Fig. 10.13 Underpinning by the insertion of an R.C. beam

3. The excavation and exposure of lengths of 1 m or less of the footings, below which a new concrete strip foundation is inserted, of greater width than the original. (See Fig. 10.14.)

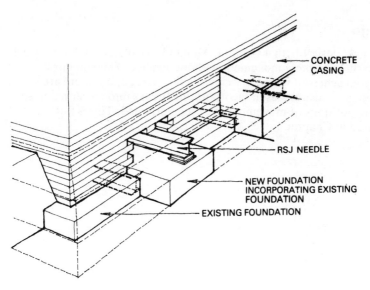

CONCRETE CASING

RSJ NEEDLE

NEW FOUNDATION INCORPORATING EXISTING FOUNDATION

EXISTING FOUNDATION

Fig. 10.14 Concrete underpinning

4. On shrinkable clay it may be desirable to insert short bored piles to provide a positive locating device for the building. (See Fig. 10.15.)

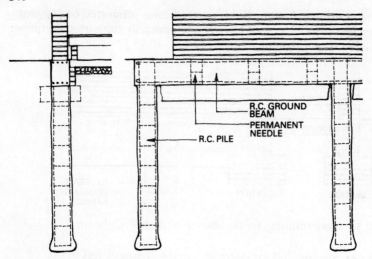

R.C. GROUND BEAM

PERMANENT NEEDLE

R.C. PILE

Fig. 10.15 Underpinning with short-bored piles may be required on shrinkable clay

Design

It is highly desirable that buildings should be designed so that they will absorb the inevitable movement without damage. This can most readily be achieved where dry construction is used, but there are considerable advantages in incorporating breaks into construction so that the positions of movement are predetermined. This is further discussed in Chapter 4.

Chapter 11

Damp

Water is one of the commonest constituents of our environment, and its presence is essential to many biological, chemical and electrical processes. Seeds require moisture for germination and both plants and animals need water for growth and the maintenance of life. However, such beneficial effects are balanced by many deleterious ones, and one of the most serious defects which can arise in a building is the presence of unwanted and uncontrolled water. Besides affecting the health of occupants, damp conditions lead to accelerated decay of many materials and unsightly staining of others, while the contents of the building may also be affected.

Steel which is in contact intermittently with water will, as described in Chapter 2, oxidise – it will rust. Other metals in similar circumstances will undergo similar processes, but the oxides are likely to produce a continuous protective coating, so that the situation is less serious in this case. On the other hand, electrolytic action between metals of widely differing potential in the presence of moisture will lead to perhaps serious staining and eventually the destruction of the baser metal. For example, aluminium will be attacked where it is in contact with mild steel in a damp atmosphere, while steel will itself be attacked in contact with copper in similar circumstances.

Where steel rusts, this may not only cause lack of strength but, because the oxide occupies more space this may actually damage a protective coating (say of concrete). Cracking of the concrete cover to steelwork, therefore, which allows water to penetrate, is likely to be followed first by orange staining and then by spalling-off of the cover. There will consequently also be a loss of fire resistance.

Fungal attack on timber (see Ch. 12) generally starts in damp, poorly ventilated conditions. Constant wetting and drying will also lead to decay of wood by the destruction of its cellular structure. Timber which is exposed therefore requires to be protected by a waterproof system of paint or varnish.

While brick and stone commonly withstand wetting without damage, the effect of freezing on wet porous materials can be to damage the interior structure, and spalling of the face can result. The erosion has to be far advanced to affect the stability of a wall to a dangerous extent, but the effect is unsightly, especially in the case of faced bricks.

A commoner defect, which is insignificant structurally but much disliked by building-owners, is the washing-out of salts contained in masonry to be deposited on the surface in the form of the white powder known as efflorescence.

Some materials, such as wood wool, lose strength when wet, and need to be protected for that reason. The thermal resistance of any structure will be reduced by being damp, as water is an excellent conductor of heat.

Internally, decorations generally show staining where damp is present, and indeed this may be one of the first signs of the existence of a problem. The adhesion of wallpapers, tiling, and floorings may be lost, and the swelling of damp wood may lead to the lifting of block floors. Mildew may appear on surfaces, especially in hidden areas such as cupboards where the evidence is not removed by regular cleaning.

Finally, the weight of water leaking into a roof space or an upper floor can be sufficient to bring down suspended ceilings.

So far as health is concerned, the main effect of dampness is accelerated heat loss. It is difficult to keep warm in a damp atmosphere because damp air is a much better conductor of heat than dry air. Cooling air due to evaporation causes discomfort, too. Additionally damp clothing may chafe and lead to rashes, and in frosty conditions damp skin is liable to chapping.

Sources of damp

The major sources of damp attacking buildings can be summarised under four headings. (See Fig. 11.1.)

Ground water (See Fig. 11.2.)

On all sites (certainly in this country) deep excavations will reveal the presence of water. Most commonly, such ground water is found within a very short depth. It will tend to seep into any excavation which is

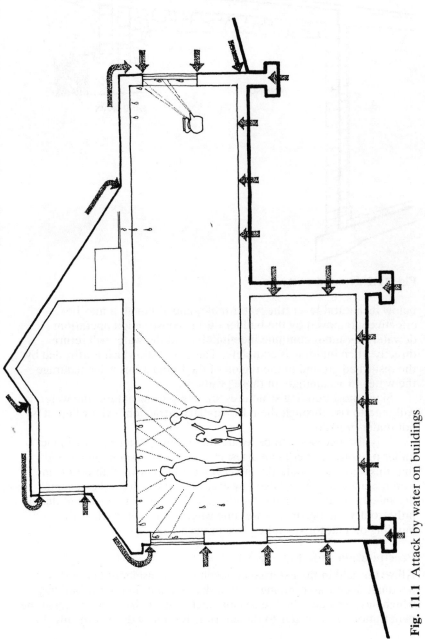

Fig. 11.1 Attack by water on buildings

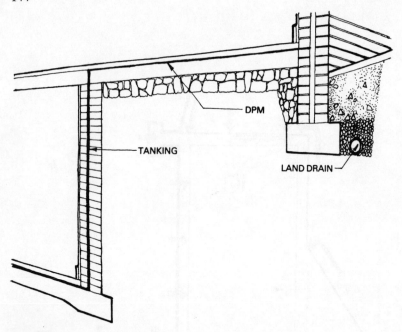

Fig. 11.2 Ground water

below its natural level (the water table) and although it may be
effectively removed by the builder during construction operations,
dewatering cannot continue indefinitely, and the water will return
directly when building is complete. The easy path which is afforded by
the disturbed ground in the region of the foundations will encourage
the water to accumulate in those positions.

Since most building structures are of a porous nature, the water
will tend to rise through them by capillary attraction, even where it is
not under pressure.

It is also necessary to be aware that ground water may be in fact
under pressure, either in an artesian basin or in a watercourse, and
that this may exacerbate the effect referred to above. Subterranean
watercourses may be changed by excavations which can be at some
distance from the particular building, and it is sometimes found that a
hitherto dry site becomes a wet one when operations such as the
building of a motorway take place in the area.

Precipitation (See Fig. 11.3.)

All water held in the external atmosphere is considered under this
heading. Such water impinges upon the external skin of the building,
which has to be designed to remain unchanged in itself and to resist the
penetration of the water to the interior. Rain may drop vertically, be

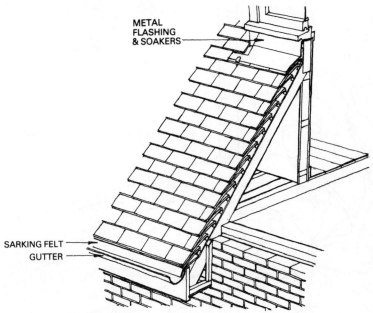

Fig. 11.3 Precipitation

blown almost horizontally by the wind or may be splashed up from the ground surface. A weight problem can be caused on roofs by a build-up of pools.

Snow may also build-up considerable weights, and may additionally become deep enough to cause penetration problems when thawing begins, of where it may be melted by warmth escaping through a wall. For example, where a lower roof abuts a higher, heated building, snow which is deeper than the flashings may cause damp in the interior of the higher building long before the thaw.

Mist and fog penetrate the smallest gaps in a structure and may cause vapour diffusion through a porous material.

Condensation (See Fig. 11.4.)

Both the water trapped in the building during construction and the water introduced into the atmosphere by the boiling of kettles and so on and the presence of breathing bodies will raise the humidity of the air. When the dewpoint temperature is reached, such humidity distils, showing as misting or running water on colder surfaces. In the case of trapped constructional water, this action may occur within the structural component, when it is known as interstitial condensation.

Leakages (See Fig. 11.5.)

It should be remembered that the many service pipes, storage tanks

Fig. 11.4 Condensation

and water-using appliances in a building are susceptible to faults. They may overflow, joints may open, or damage may occur due to movement or frost. Many signs of damp can be traced to such sources.

Whenever evidence of damp is discovered, usually in the form of staining, though sometimes in the form of visible saturation, an attempt has to be made to determine the source of the water. It is often necessary to carry out quite extensive tests with moisture meters to determine the extent of the problem, and to make a thoughtful analytical examination of the whole structure. If leakage is suspected, it may be possible to confirm this by introducing a stain into the suspect source.

Damp is often a symptom of an underlying fault. For example, differential settlement may fracture a DPC, with consequent damp patches showing as staining of internal decorations. The settlement may have had far-reaching effects, which need to be evaluated. (See Ch. 10.)

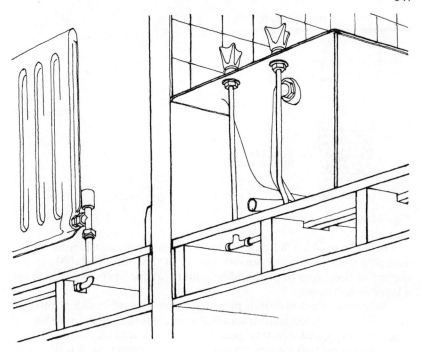

Fig. 11.5 Leaks

Defences against damp in modern buildings

Modern buildings are designed and constructed specifically to prevent the adverse effects of damp.

Ground water

On particularly wet sites it is usual to employ land drains to remove excess water from the vicinity of the building. Figure 11.6 shows that these may be in the form of open-jointed pipes or of rubble-filled trenches surrounding the building and laid to a gentle gradient so as to encourage the flow of the water to a rubble-filled hollow, or soakaway. Although such measures will remove a proportion of the water from the site, it is still always necessary to introduce an absolute barrier to the upward migration of water through the structure of the building, in the form of a DPC. Where the ground floor is suspended this is generally considered an adequate defence, provided all timbers are above DPC level and the space below the ground floor is ventilated. Water may well penetrate to the upper surface of the oversite concrete, but will be dissipated on the air current. Lack of ventilation would produce dangerously damp conditions in this situation.

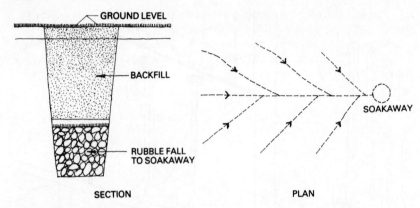

Fig. 11.6 Land drains

In the case of a solid ground floor, it is generally considered desirable to incorporate a positive barrier in the form of a DPM across the entire floor area of the building, and to lay the oversite concrete on a layer of hardcore.

Where accommodation is provided below ground level a positive vertical barrier in the wall structure also becomes essential, and the whole underground structure generally has to be tanked.

Bituminous tanking will provide complete protection, if it is properly carried out, but needs to be protected itself both from mechanical damage and from being forced away from the wall and floor by the effect of water pressure. It is usually recommended that it should be applied to the outer surface of the structure for the greatest effect, and protected by a further layer of 100 mm concrete or a half-brick wall. An alternative is the incorporation into concrete of a proprietary chemical waterproofer, but it is difficult to ensure that this has been satisfactorily spread throughout the mix, and the effect may be largely psychological, causing greater care in mixing than usual.

Precipitation

As much as possible of the water from precipitation is led away by providing falls to surfaces and a system of gutters and rainwater pipes. Whether such gutters are integral to a roof or of the prefabricated bracketed type, the maintenance of free flow is essential if they are to remain effective. Flashings are generally provided to protect the vulnerable joints of a roof structure.

Experiments have been made with completely flat roofs, the idea being to allow the water to stand, but in practice it has proved almost impossible to achieve and maintain a totally flat surface, and pooling of the water seems inevitable. The action of the sun on puddles leads to differential thermal movement in the roof covering, which can result in fracture.

The detailed design of components such as windows is devised to shed water rapidly. As well as sloping surfaces, drips are incorporated where droplets of water drawn along a surface will accumulate until the weight is sufficient for the moisture to drip down to ground clear of the wall surface. The window detail in Fig. 11.7 shows the care with which such problems are tackled.

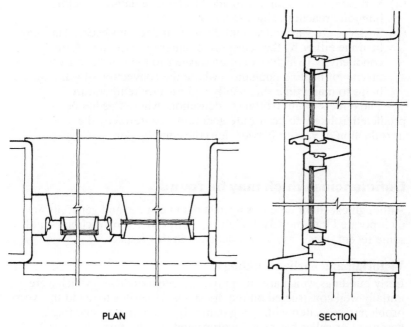

PLAN   SECTION

Fig. 11.7 Defences in the window against water penetration

Apart from some roof finishes few of the materials of construction are totally waterproof (though the use of plastics and other impervious materials is increasing). Generally, however, the passage of water through structures is prevented by one of the following means.

(a) The structure may be made so thick that, although water penetrates deep into it, it dries before it reaches the inner surface. This is a mechanism suitable to a climate where rainfall is intermittent, such as our own, but demands walls, for example, much thicker than would be required for structural reasons.

(b) A completely water-resistant barrier may be incorporated into the structure.

(c) A cavity may be included as a positive defence against the entry of moisture.

The cavity wall, as it is commonly used, combines (b) and (c) to provide complete protection of the interior from damp while the weight of the structure is minimised.

The importance of a good paint system to protect timber and steel from the effects of damp must not be forgotten. (See Ch. 7.)

Condensation

The effects of condensation can be eradicated by two alternative strategies. Either

(a) Sufficient ventilation is provided to remove damp air before humidity reaches danger level; or

(b) Surfaces are warmed so that distillation does not occur. This may be done either by the selection of materials with low thermal conductivity (which tend to be warmer to the touch) or by the placing of heating appliances where the convection of warm air helps to maintain a sufficiently high surface temperature.

The effects of interstitial condensation, where this has been predicted as likely to occur, are generally countered by the introduction of vapour barriers into the construction.

Deficiencies which may be found

Although excellent defences against damp can be, and generally are, incorporated into modern buildings, many older constructions – and some recent ones – are in fact deficient in this respect.

Victorian and earlier buildings

Early buildings which are still in use are generally those which were initially well constructed on the driest available sites to avoid the worst problems associated with rising damp. It is common to find that a basement or cellar has been incorporated so as to raise the main habitable rooms above the level at which they would be most vulnerable. The cellars themselves are often damp, and though intended as store places may not be suitable for this purpose. Damp proof courses, generally in the form of two courses of blue bricks or of slates are found towards the end of the period and cellars then tend to disappear.

Walls are usually constructed from solid masonry, and may not be sufficiently thick to resist the penetration of persistent rain. Where they are rendered in the attempt to provide a watertight coating, crazing and spalling often impair the effectiveness of the cement rendering.

Roofs are generally steeply pitched and often served by lead-lined gutters, which may be found to have become brittle with age and to show cracking, and flashings may be similarly defective. Cast-iron rainwater goods may have rusted, and in particular the bolts fixing rainwater pipes to walls have often decayed. It is unusual to find any underlay or sarking to a roof covering of slates or tiles though there may be unprotected boarding, which is very vulnerable to damp. Rain and snow may be blown into roof cavities in strong wind conditions. This may not be a serious defect, providing the space is adequately ventilated.

Early framed buildings sometimes have defective detailing where cladding meets frame, and since it is unusual for expansion joints to have been included, water may enter where differential thermal movement has caused cracking. Damp also frequently penetrates buildings of this age through cracks caused by differential settlement. (See Ch. 10.)

Edwardian buildings

In the first decades of the present century, much sound building work was performed, which is still in excellent condition. Solid walls were still the norm.

Much timber which has not been maintained in good decorative repair in buildings of this age may be found to have decayed, and this may particularly be the case where projecting windows are found.

While DPCs were by no means universal, basements and cellars virtually disappeared from houses, which frequently suffer from damp at ground level. Below-ground accommodation in commercial buildings is common, and though this may have been adequately tanked when built it may now show defects in the waterproofing. Cast-iron drainage may be evident in such basements, and may show signs of deterioration.

Inter-war building

The cavity wall became common during the inter-war period in house construction, but many buildings (including some houses) were built with single brick walls and rendered, which now show considerable penetration by damp. Damp proof courses are not universal.

However, it is at the junctions between structures that the greatest problems are to be expected, and the detailing of eaves, lintols, bay windows and entrance doors often shows a faulty appreciation of the effects of water attack. Flashings may be missing.

It is common, too, for alterations made to such buildings to have bridged DPCs and cavities and so have introduced problems not present originally.

The permanent ventilation which originally protected such buildings from the effects of condensation may have been blocked – in particular, fireplaces have often been removed without leaving ventilation to flues – and low standards of thermal insulation provide conditions where condensation is likely.

Post-war

Most post-war buildings are well defended against attack by water, but bridged cavities, faulty cavity trays, and bridged DPCs may be discovered, often resulting from rushed workmanship. By far the commonest problem, however, is due to condensation. Modern building materials, particularly internal finishes, tend to be impervious and cold to the touch, and concrete and steel frames conduct heat more readily than brick or stone masonry. These cold surfaces are conducive to condensation. Additionally, the level of heating demanded by occupants has risen, while the general level of ventilation has dropped – since it seems extravagant in an era of high energy costs to allow the escape of expensively heated air. The moisture content of the air is high, while the surfaces it contacts are cold. Condensation results on a wider scale than had hitherto been usual. This is frequently mistaken for moisture penetration, since it occurs in places other than those where condensation had traditionally been expected. Careful investigation is often needed to determine the true source of the water. Interstitial condensation is also an increasing problem – in concrete roofs, for example – resulting in invisible but insidious deterioration.

In buildings of any age, the main danger signs include damp patches (which may show as loss of adhesion of wallpaper, stained decorations or dark marks, as well as patches that are actually damp to the touch) as follows.

(a) Internal staining to a fairly even level around the external walls of a building, probably indicating the absence or failure of the DPC.

(b) Patches of staining to the interior of walls at low level, which probably indicate local bridging of the DPC.

(c) Patches at the points where two different constructions meet, indicating faulty detailing, with the probable absence of a DPC.

(d) Damp-staining round window openings in cavity construction, which may indicate the absence of a proper DPC, or faulty placing.

(e) Random damp patches to the inner face of external walls, which may result from mortar droppings lodged on cavity ties providing a bridge for water.

(f) Damp patches in the interior at about eaves level, indicating either faulty eaves construction or a blocked gutter causing constant saturation of the wall.

(g) Damp patches behind rainwater heads, indicating blocked rainwater pipes.

(h) Patches to ceilings, indicating either missing roof covering or flashings or leaking services.
    It should be noted that water entering the building may travel along a structure, and will not necessarily show itself directly behind its point of entry.

(i) Damp patches on the surface of colder structures, which are likely to be caused by condensation, especially if wet window-cills show evidence of water running down glass.

Remedies

The major remedies required might include those referred to briefly below, but every case needs, of course, to be treated on its merits. It is essential to first determine and eradicate the cause of the water penetration, before treating symptoms.

Making-good roof covering

It is usually a simple matter to replace individual slates or tiles or to recover roofs covered with these materials where a considerable number of units is missing or damaged. In the latter case, the opportunity to ensure that adequate sarking is present can be taken. 'Torching' – the cement pointing of tiled roofs – is sometimes advocated to extend the life of defective tiles. This is difficult to recommend, as inevitable movement due to loading and heat is bound to result in hair cracks, through which water will be attracted by capillary action. If tiles are so decayed (usually as a result of frost action or moss) that they no longer provide a generally water-resistant covering, they should be replaced.

Frequently a major fault lies in flashings which may be loose (needing to be tucked home and re-wedged) or fractured (when replacement will be necessary). All flashings should rise at least 150 mm above the surface as a protection against lying snow.

Coverings to flat roofs may need to be completely stripped and replaced as repairs often do little more than remove a problem to a different location. Fifteen years is frequently quoted as the useful life of a built-up bituminous roofing system. Other problems may be associated with bubbling and blistering beneath an impervious surface due to trapped water. This may result in difficulty with the run-off of water, and differential thermal expansion in the surface, causing cracking. Screeds, especially lightweight ones, should be ventilated to avoid this problem.

Care always has to be taken, when waterproofing a roof, to avoid sealing-off the ventilation to timber structures.

Rendering to walls

Solid walls which, because they are particularly exposed, are frequently penetrated by rain, may have their performance improved by raking out the horizontal joints of brickwork, or rough-hammering concrete, to provide a key (or using a proprietary bonder) and applying a rough-cast rendering. This type of coating is always to be preferred to the denser, but more vulnerable to cracking, stuccos when applied for waterproofing.

A more satisfactory expedient may lie in the addition of weather boarding or tile-hanging, which do not suffer from the disadvantages of doubtful adhesion and high maintenance associated with many renderings.

Pointing brickwork can be helpful if the joints are badly eroded, but should not be thought of in isolation as a panacea for damp walls, and painting and invisible silicone applications are of temporary effect, requiring regular attention to retain their usefulness.

It is rarely useful to apply any kind of waterproofing to the inner surface of walls, as this will fail to withstand water pressure.

Inserting a DPC

Three principal ways of inserting a DPC are generally recognised as follows.

(a) Cut through horizontal joints and insert a DPC of the conventional type, in short lengths. As can be seen from Fig. 11.8, this is a laborious and time-consuming operation, and it is expensive. Undoubtedly good results are produced.

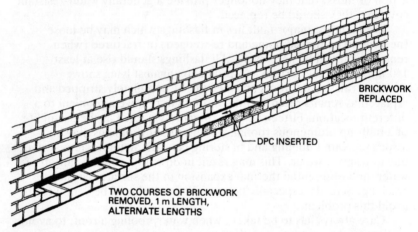

BRICKWORK REPLACED

DPC INSERTED

TWO COURSES OF BRICKWORK REMOVED, 1 m LENGTH, ALTERNATE LENGTHS

Fig. 11.8 Insertion of DPC

(b) Inject a chemical damp-proofer into the structure. A disadvantage is that such an injection is invisible, and it is impossible to establish how satisfactory a job has been done until it is tested by wet conditions. For this reason, it is often necessary to resort to overkill so as to be certain that a good result is achieved.

(c) The installation of an electric circuit making use of the potential of the materials and the earth to repel water by production of an electric field. However unlikely this may sound, it is said to produce very satisfactory results, though it has barely been in use for long enough to make certain that the effect is permanent. Installation is simple and very speedy, and there is no connection to the mains or to batteries.

There is also a system which uses the same principle on which land drainage depends. That is, it provides an easy path for the water to lead it from the structure, by inserting short pipes into the wall. This can most suitably be used in connection with (b) above.

Provision of tanking (See Fig. 11.9.)

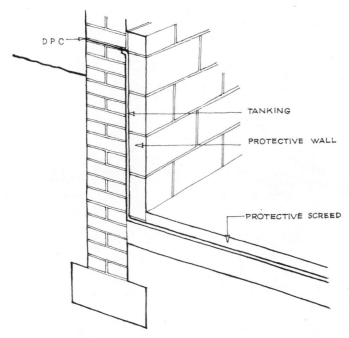

Fig. 11.9 Addition of tanking

Where it is necessary to tank an existing basement it is not of course practicable to apply the treatment to the outer surface. It is therefore necessary to apply two coats of bitumen to the inner surface of walls and floor and to protect this with a structure sufficiently heavy to withstand the water pressure. The painting of waterproofing compound alone to such surfaces is unlikely to be a long-term solution to the problem. If, however, there is no sign of damp in the basement excepting that paper becomes very slightly soft, compounds or polythene linings may be acceptable provided they are protected from mechanical damage. A careful watch should be kept for signs of failure.

Redecoration
Redecoration to maintain a faultless waterproofing on timber and steel is often the most important action to be taken against damp. Since it is

the integrity of the entire paint system which provides the protection, it is often best to leave in place all paint which is not loose, but care should be taken to ensure that drips and water checks do not become filled with paint.

For remedial action where fungal attack is present, see Chapter 12.

Chapter 12

Biological attack on timber

As has been pointed out in Chapter 2, timber is one of the commonest materials used in building because of its wide availability and because stocks are renewable. It suffers, however, from the disadvantage of being among the materials most vulnerable to decay. It is essential to understand the sources of attack, the conditions in which they flourish, and the means available to avoid and to combat infestation.

The commonest causes of failure in buildings include attack by fungal growths and by insects. In either case, the trouble is liable to arise in structural timbers which are not under continuous observation, and the conditions for an attack are as likely to result from neglect of proper maintenance as from faulty original detailing or construction.

Attacks of these kinds often pass unnoticed until they are well advanced and considerable damage has been caused. Detection in the early stages is difficult unless suspicion has been aroused, perhaps because of an attack in adjacent property.

Fungal attack

Students should note that the scientific names of many of the fungi which attack timber in buildings have been changed fairly recently. Older editions of many standard textbooks will be found to contain the superceded names, which are therefore mentioned below to avoid confusion.

Dry Rot (*serpula lachrymans*, formerly *merulius lachrymans*)

Dry rot is a living organism, which needs food, moisture and oxygen if it is to survive. The popular name is derived from the very dessicated nature of the wood left after an attack. Characteristically such timber is very dry and exhibits a rectangular structure. (See Fig. 12.1.)

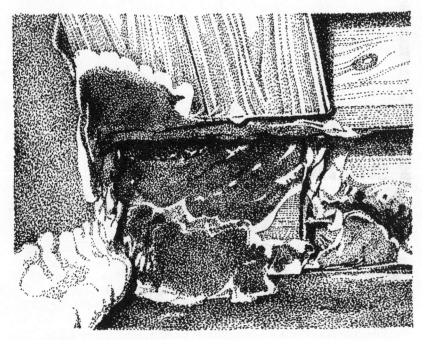

Fig. 12.1 Dry rot, *serpula lachrymans*

A fruiting body, or sporophore, which is unlike that of the familiar mushroom or toadstool in that it has no stalk, can release spores into the air in very large numbers over a period of many days when it is mature. Tens of thousands of spores per hour may originate from each square centimetre of the hymenium or fruiting surface.

Such spores are, individually, invisible, but in these enormous quantities appear as a brick-red dust. They are very light, and easily blown about by the wind. Those which reach damp softwoods in unventilated conditions germinate, putting out rootlike threads called hyphae through which to feed, which eventually build-up into a cotton wool-like mass known as mycelium. The hyphae may seek deep into the structure of the wood for the cellulose on which the fungus feeds, and in this case it will be hard to find evidence of the presence of mycelium. Quite often, however, the mat stretches across the surface, and it may look like a skin or like cotton wool.

Timber from which the cellulose has been extracted, and into which the hyphae have penetrated deeply, has its essential structure broken down, resulting in severe loss of strength. When the fungus is well established, strands may riddle masonry, and damp may be conveyed along them to allow previously dry timber to be colonised.

As maturity is reached, fruiting bodies are formed. These may reach anything up to 2 m in diameter, and they have a distinctive leathery red surface with white or yellowish edges.

The fungus is virulent, and remedial action is essential directly the existence of an attack is confirmed.

The claim to be able to recognise the presence of dry rot by a characteristic odour is challenged by botanists: it seems more plausible that the damp, unventilated conditions which favour growth give rise to an easily recognised smell. Signs which should lead to suspicion of infection include such fusty conditions, the presence of timber in damp, ill-ventilated spaces, visible mycelium and dry, almost friable timber, as well as the obvious presence of sporophores.

Specialist firms are usually prepared to make diagnostic surveys without charge. Competitive quotations can (and probably should) be obtained – but there ought to be a minimum of delay in putting the full action recommended by the specialists into effect.

This will in all probability involve the removal of all obviously infected timber and that within about 600 mm of the attack, all of which should be burnt on site. Masonry in the vicinity will need to be sterilised, either with temperatures of the order of 40 °C maintained for 15 minutes (a dangerous expedient which may well result in fire) or with a potent water-based fungicide such as sodium pentachlorophenate. Replacement timbers must have been protected by pressure-impregnation with fungicide.

Clearly all this would be useless unless the source of damp were also dealt with, and good ventilation ensured. Otherwise the possible resurgence of a dormant growth could not be excluded.

It is usual for a firm which carries out remedial work after an attack of dry rot to provide a guarantee against recurrence of the growth within a stated period. This will not, of course, indemnify the owner if his maintenance is negligent – if he allows damp, unventilated conditions to build-up again, for example. Neither will he usually be covered if an attack, hitherto unsuspected, is found in a different part of his property, even if that area was inspected during the initial survey.

It should also be recognised that a thirty-year guarantee is only of any value if the firm in question remains in business for that length of time, unless some special arrangement with a trade organisation for continuity of cover has been made.

Wet rot (Cellar fungus) (*coniophora puteana*, formerly *coniophora cerebella*)

Wet rots are found in wood with a water content between 21 and 40 per cent and timber which has been damaged may show longitudinal but not cross-cracking. Often, though, the damage is internal, and hidden within a thin casing of sound wood. The sheet-like sporophores are greenish to olive in colour, and the spores are borne in small pimples on the surface. The hyphae are yellowish, and may darken to brown or nearly black, and the fruiting body may be surrounded by spidery mycelium. The spores, if found in quantity, look like khaki dust.

Unlike dry rot, wet rot does not produce strands able to conduct moisture to hitherto dry wood, and for this reason this is considered to be a less dangerous condition and easier to eradicate.

Treatment generally involves removal of the original source of the damp, and removal of damaged timber, which is replaced with treated members.

Poria (*Fibroporia vaillantii*, formerly *poria vaillantii*)

A fungus which may be difficult to distinguish from dry rot, poria is found in very wet situations. The fruiting body and mycelium is white, without any of the rich colour of *serpula lachrymans*. Poria may spread from saturated softwoods to wet hardwoods, but does not attack dry timbers.

Paxillus (*Paxillus panuoides*)

This fungus may be confused with wet rot, but the fruiting bodies have an unusual branching shape, and the decaying wood is often bright yellow.

Phellinus (*Phellinus cryptarum*)

Phellinus attacks oak in particular, and the damage may be internal and unnoticed until the brown sporophores appear. The mycelium is thick and yellow brown, and a yellowish exudation is often found. Timber attacked by phellinus is said to be particularly vulnerable to further attack by the death watch beetle.

Phellinus is a 'white' rot, which destroys the lignum as well as the cellulose in timber.

Other fungi

A number of other fungi which may attack structural timbers has been distinguished. It is important that identification should be made by a specialist, so that the most appropriate treatment can be applied.

Moulds and mildew

Other moulds, which indicate the presence of damp but do no structural damage may appear as dark spots or as a slight furriness of the surface. These can usually be controlled by washing with an anti-fungal wash or household bleach. The source of damp should, of course, be found and eradicated, and where the blotching occurs on decorated surfaces it may be desirable to remove the decorations, thoroughly dry out the structure, and then redecorate with fungicidal materials.

Woodboring insects

The life-cycle of all woodboring insects is similar.

Eggs are laid in surface cracks of the timber, and when the grubs or larvae (erroneously referred to as 'woodworm') hatch out, they bore down into the depth of the wood, devouring the cellulose in the sapwood which is their food, while expelling debris, or 'frass'. Frass may be the first sign of an attack, and is also an important aid in identifying the particular species present.

When it is fully grown, the larva excavates a nest, or chamber, just below the surface of the wood, in which it pupates. Eventually it develops into an adult beetle which emerges from the surface leaving a characteristic flight hole, commonly on the underside of the member.

Timber may be seriously damaged by the tunnelling larvae long before exit holes are caused and the infestation noticed, but in this country the damage is rarely if ever sufficiently serious to cause structural collapse.

Furniture beetle (*Anobium punctatum*)

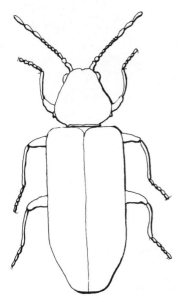

Fig. 12.2 Furniture beetle, *anobium punctatum*

This insect may attack both hardwoods and softwoods, as well as plywood and wickerwork, and is the commonest wood-boring pest in buildings in this country. Larvae may infest dry wood for periods of over three years, so that latent and unsuspected infection may be brought into buildings in apparently sound wood, including furniture.

The frass is sandy in texture, and the regular, round, exit holes are about 2 mm in diameter.

Death watch beetle (*Xestobium rufovillosum*)

This long-lived insect, whose life-cycle may last considerably beyond the usual three-years in sound timber, is particularly likely to attack old or decayed hardwood in poorly ventilated conditions. There are bun-shaped fragments in the frass which are large enough to be visible. Flight holes are larger than those of the furniture beetle, at 3 mm diameter, and a ticking noise can be heard at times. This is a mating cry.

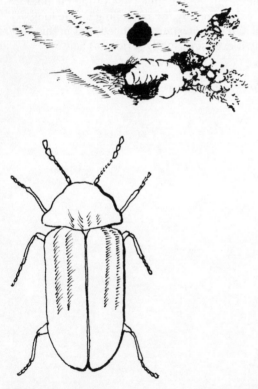

Fig. 12.3 Death watch beetle, *xestobium rufovillosum*

House longhorn beetle (*Hylotrupes bajulus*)

Though widespread on the Continent, this pest has at present been identified only in a limited area of the Home Counties in this country. The larvae can do extensive damage to structural members before the presence of the insect is suspected, and special precautions are in force in the affected district. The beetle is large, and the oval flight holes may have the larger dimension as great as 9.5 mm, while the debris is in the form of cylindrical fragments.

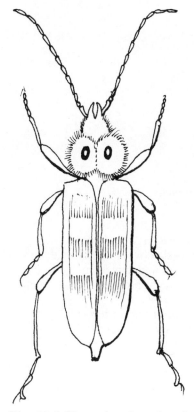

Fig. 12.4 House longhorn beetle, *hylotrupes bajulus*

Powder post beetle (*Lyctus brunneus*)

This insect attacks the sapwood of hardwoods if they have an open texture and are starchy. Floury powder is found, and the flight hole is about 1.6 mm in diameter. Beech and birch are too fine-pored to be vulnerable, and older timber is less likely to be attacked than new.

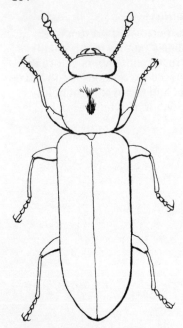

Fig. 12.5 Powder post beetle, *lyctus brunneus*

Other beetles

The evidence of the presence of other insects may be confused with symptoms of the dangerous ones mentioned above. For example, weevils attack very damp and decayed wood and leave damage similar to that of the furniture beetle, though the flight holes may be as small as 0.8 mm in diameter.

As in the case of fungal attack, it is important for a correct diagnosis of the insect responsible for damage to timber to be made by an expert, so that correct and immediate treatment can be effected.

Treatment

The first step in treatment is to remove all dust and debris, usually by suction, and cut out all timber so severely damaged as to be no longer structurally sound. All remaining timber must be impregnated with insecticide, and new timber which is introduced should be pressure-treated.

Woodworm may be destroyed by high, sustained, temperatures, but a chlorinated hydrocarbon insecticide, in an organic solvent which will be readily absorbed into the timber is more generally advocated.

A specialist firm which carries out remedial work will normally give a guarantee against recurrence of the same trouble in the treated area. The reservations expressed with regard to guarantees against recurrence of fungal attack apply here, too.

A combined insecticide and fungicide may be used.

It should be noted that all the potent chemicals used to combat biological attack on timber may be dangerously toxic to people and their pets, and may carry a fire risk during application. They must be used carefully and under controlled conditions. The British Wood Preserving Association will advise on appropriate safety precautions.

Avoiding an attack

Since, as described above, the treatment once a biological attack is discovered is likely to be draconian, it is clearly preferable to take preventative action.

The careful specification of materials and detailing of their application is obviously a priority in this respect. Imported hardwoods may carry latent beetle infestation, and rapid seasoning may prevent detection before the timber is used. All such timbers should be subjected to careful examination.

The pressure impregnation of all structural timbers with a fungicidal and insecticidal preservative has much to recommend it.

Careful detailing to avoid the creation of damp unventilated cavities, as seen in the details of faults shown in Fig. 12.6(a), is

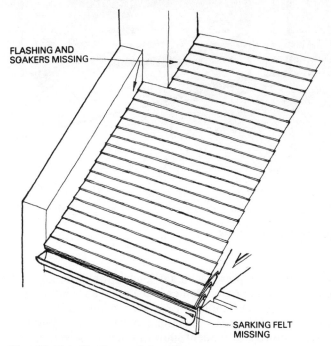

FLASHING AND SOAKERS MISSING

SARKING FELT MISSING

Fig. 12.6(a) Faulty roof detailing

essential. Twenty per cent moisture content favours dry rot, which cannot, however, spread to very wet timber, though wet rot can.

Supervision of construction to ensure accuracy in placing DPCs, cavity trays and other precautions against the penetration of damp, and the provision of unobstructed ventilation to roofs and below suspended ground floors, is clearly of the greatest importance.

Maintenance

In existing buildings, regular inspections of all structural timbers should be made, and care should be taken to avoid the blocking of necessary air bricks and the bridging of DPCs, which is sometimes caused by the build-up of flowerbeds around a building.

The maintenance of a good paint system on joinery is essential as a precaution against decay. (See Fig. 12.6(b).)

Fig. 12.6(b) Decay due to wetting

Infection

Anyone who has been in the presence of any kind of fungal attack should take care to shake out outer clothes in the open air, and wash shoes before entering another building, to avoid carrying the infection into other property. In extreme cases, clothing may have to be burnt.

Second-hand furniture is a frequent source of beetle infestation, and all should be inspected carefully for live attack, and treated before being brought into the house (by injection of insecticide into flight holes) if there is any doubt. It should be noted that where the wood surface within holes is as dark as the outer surface, this indicates an old attack, which has in all probability been treated or died out of its own accord, but that old flight holes are sometimes selected as spots in which to lay new eggs.

Chapter 13

Dirt

Traces of any unwanted material upon any other can properly and reasonably be regarded as dirt, but it is more practical to consider only those deposits which have, in one way or another, harmful effects as soiling. This definition will include the following.
(a) Chemical deposits from fumes.
(b) Dust and grit from the erosion of other surfaces, including animal hair.
(c) Grease and oil from mineral sources.
(d) Animal and bird droppings.
(e) Food particles.

Their harmful effects may be purely aesthetic or may affect health, and might include the following.
(a) The multiplication of bacteria in organic compounds, with consequent risks to health.
(b) Chemical attack upon building materials, leading to loss of strength, erosion or staining.
(c) Physical erosion by airborne grit or by grit carried on the feet.
(d) Encouragement of the germination and growth of lichens and moulds in pockets of earth.
(e) Discoloration. It should be noted, however, that not all authorities agree that buildings are improved in appearance by being cleaned. Some buildings are considered to be enhanced by pattern staining which emphasises such features as cornices and stringcourses, and to look excessively bland when cleaned.

This is not an appropriate place to discuss the organisation or methodology of housekeeping. A great deal can, however, be done by thoughtful design to minimise the need for regular maintenance of interiors. Eighty per cent of the dirt entering buildings is said to do so on people's feet and much of this quantity can be eliminated by attention to such points as the following.

(a) If a building is arranged so that people entering it do so after crossing an area of well-drained hardstanding, much dirt will be removed from their shoes as they do so.

(b) The installation of gridded footscrapers across which entrants must walk will remove most of the residual grit and mud from their footwear. The use of coconut-matting should be avoided, as it rapidly becomes saturated with mud and is difficult to clean. Hard rubber slotted mats are to be preferred.

It should also be borne in mind that many activities carried on in buildings are inherently dirt-creating, and buildings should be designed to minimise the extent to which the resulting mess is spread around the building. Such areas should, firstly, be arranged as self-contained and isolated suites. Secondly, materials should be chosen and details devised which allow for easy and regular cleaning.

The installation of vacuum systems is helpful in encouraging thorough cleaning.

The design of hyperclean areas, such as operating suites or laboratories is beyond the scope of this book.

Weathering

External building surfaces weather because of the action of trace elements in rainwater or the atmosphere, because of erosion by airborne grit, because salt in a seaside atmosphere attracts moisture or by the action of frost. Not all weathering is harmful: the patina formed on copper is an example of beneficent weathering. Stone in particular can decay if deposits of dirt are allowed to accummulate.

A variety of acids and alkalis in weak solution in the atmosphere can cause damage to varying extents, but the most important is thought to be sulphur dioxide resulting from smoke which attacks the matrix or binding agent in the stone.

The cleaning of stonework, particularly where dirt has resulted from decades of smoke pollution, is frequently recommended, especially where, because of smokeless zones, the blackening is unlikely to recur.

The choice of method is critical, as it is possible to do extensive damage by injudicious cleaning, and all cleaning is liable to do at least some damage. The advice of a specialist firm – and not one which specialises in a single cleaning method – should be sought, and it is often advisable to experiment on an unobtrusive area of the surface if there is any doubt.

Owners of buildings scheduled as ancient monuments have to give notice to the Department of the Environment before putting cleaning in hand. They are advised to first seek the advice of their local Planning Officer.

Bird droppings contain soluble salts and also encourage bacterial growth (though this is not today considered to be a significant factor in stone decay). Persistent pecking causes subtle erosion and the droppings are unsightly. For these reasons owners are often anxious to discourage birds, particularly starlings and pigeons, from roosting on their buildings. The most effective method seems to be painting horizontal ledges with special paint on which the birds cannot gain a foothold.

Methods of cleaning stonework

Water spray

Spraying of water, with a jet which is controllable both in velocity and volume, is the gentlest available method of cleaning and the least likely to damage masonry. It is slow, but a quiet and cheap procedure, which is often suitable for use on limestone. It is harmless to operatives and causes little public nuisance. There are, however, certain disadvantages. The wall may become saturated, so that internal finishes are damaged, and timber and steel built into the wall may be affected. There is also some slight danger of drain blockage. More seriously, stains may appear on limestone, especially Portland stone, later. These are due to soluble matter from soot being driven deep into the structure of the stone by the jets, to migrate later when the wall is again wetted by rain and appear on the surface. Such stains may disappear spontaneously, though this is by no means general.

Water spray cannot, because of the danger of frost damage, be used in wintry weather.

The water is used to soften the dirt, which is usually removed by brushes or other mechanical means, though it may sometimes be washed away by the jets. Only experiment can tell how long it will take for particular deposits to soften, and the time may be considerable.

Steam

The use of steam for cleaning is more or less obsolete since it is not proved to be more effective than water. The problems associated with water spray are paralleled, though the effects are less severe because less water is used. There is an additional danger of scalding to the workmen. Steam-cleaning is more expensive than water spray, but may be useful to remove spot stains left after acid cleaning. As with water spray, the steam softens the dirt, which is largely removed by mechanical means.

Dry grit blasting

Dry grit blasting is expensive and potentially injurious to the health of operatives, who should wear respirators. It is noisy and dusty and there is considerable danger that drains may get blocked. The whole work area needs to be close-sheeted for protection, and all the openings in the building must be sealed. Skill is needed to avoid surface damage, especially to fine features, and the method is usually only recommended for use on hard stones, particularly sandstones which cannot be cleaned effectively with water, though highly controlled techniques now make the process usable on limestone. The surface of limestone will be roughened, and more likely to accumulate new deposits of dirt.

Dry grit blasting is quick and can be used in all weather conditions.

Wet grit blasting

This technique uses less water than a water spray and generates less injurious dust than dry blasting. It is fast but expensive, and it carries an increased risk of drain blockage, and limestone may be stained. It is said to be disliked by workmen, who are liable to turn off the water unless they are well supervised.

Mechanical cleaning

At any season of the year mechanical means on their own can be used to clean masonry, and there are none of the dangers associated with the use of water. Discs, brushes or steel wire may be used, and the process is fast, though expensive. There is considerable danger of damage to the surface, particularly to fine detail, and the method is most applicable to plain areas of ashlar. There is serious danger and nuisance from dust, and workpeople have to wear eye protection and airline helmets.

Hydrofluoric acid

Though most chemical cleaners should be avoided, because they either contain or cause the deposit of soluble salts, the use of hydrofluoric acid to clean sandstones is satisfactory. The material is dangerous, both to the operatives, who must wear protective cloth clothing to avoid painful skin burns, and to polished materials and glass which can be instantly etched. Extreme care in using the method is therefore essential, and it should be attempted only by properly trained workmen.

Ammonium bifluoride is recommended only for the cleaning of granite, which can, however, generally be satisfactorily washed.

Copper stains can be removed from stone with a poultice of

whiting in ammonia, which is brushed off when dry, or with a solution of ammonia, and oil stains can be removed with carbon tetrachloride. Iron stains can be removed from Portland stone with water and brush. No attempt should ever be made to clean brickwork, excepting to wash-off smoke stains after fire damage, because of the danger of irrevocable damage to the surface.

Chapter 14

Alterations

If it is well designed, soundly built and conscientiously maintained, the natural life of a building should be considerable. One hundred years is certainly not an unreasonable expectation of useful existence for a factory building or house, while many public buildings and churches several centuries old are still in daily, and efficient, use. Buildings become outdated for two principal reasons.

1. People's expectations of the level of performance of buildings in keeping out the weather, conserving energy, providing useful levels of natural light and so on are constantly raised as new buildings capable of achieving higher standards are provided. Because a new building can provide a higher standard of thermal insulation, say, than could be expected of an older, one, the latter begins to be considered obsolete.

2. When the way of life or process that a building was designed to accommodate is outmoded, the building becomes redundant. The almost universal penetration of household television makes the neighbourhood cinema obsolete, or changing educational philosophy demands the abandonment of neighbourhood schools. In either case a perfectly sound building may be left untenanted.

Buildings in either of these categories represent a considerable capital investment as well as being an important part of the man-made environment many wish to conserve. There is a natural desire to re-use such structures by adapting them to new uses wherever this is possible: this should not however be attempted without adequate forethought. The cost of an adapted building may be as great as that of building from new foundations, while the facilities provided may be inferior. This has to be balanced carefully against the advantage of preserving cherished buildings.

Selecting a building for conversion

The purpose for which the adapted building is to be used will of course, be one for which a need is known to exist. There is little point in adapting a Beechinged branch railway station to be a pub, because the accommodation looks suitable, if the neighbourhood is already over-provided in this respect.

Fig. 14.1 Buildings become obsolete before they wear out

The need to match the existing building with its proposed use may be of the greatest significance in the case of an owner who wishes to put premises to profitable use after their first purpose is outworn. Careful calculation is necessary to ensure that it is in fact advantageous to adapt in comparison with either demolition and new building or sale of the property and purchase or building elsewhere. (See Fig. 14.2.)

Site

The most important factor affecting the suitability of premises for a particular adaptation is undoubtedly the siting. This is the one feature which it is (in all normal circumstances) quite impossible to alter. It is vital to ensure that the adapted building will be suitably sited in relation to other developments, access and services. The charm or suitability of the building on other grounds should not be allowed to blind the developer or his advisers to deficiences in this respect. The

Fig. 14.2 A new use can often be found

degree of care should not be inferior to that which would be expended on the selection of a greenfield site.

It is important, naturally, to establish by enquiry at the planning office that there is no obstacle to the intended use on the grounds of zoning regulations or other planning constraints.

Accommodation

It is obviously important that there should be a good match between the accommodation required for the new use and the enclosed space afforded by the structure. The potential ways in which this can be subdivided, both horizontally and vertically, need to be explored: space above a reasonable ceiling height which cannot be brought into use as an upper floor, while having to be heated, is a positive disadvantage. On the other hand, imaginative three-dimensional design can sometimes exploit an unpromising section to good advantage, and a building need not be lightly discarded before the possibilities of fitting in all the needed accommodation have been thoroughly investigated.

Structure

Unless the structure of the selected building is basically sound it might be an extravagance to attempt to prolong its useful life. A structural survey is essential, not only to establish the means by which the loads are transferred to the foundations (so that this can be taken into account during design) but also to identify defects which require attention. The cost of putting the structure into good order must be taken into account in evaluating the viability of the scheme.

For many purposes a space covered by a single span, or at least a small number of large spans, will prove more adaptable than one planned on a cellular basis, with many loadbearing internal partitions. Any alteration involving considerable structural work is likely to prove uneconomic.

Services

The availability of services is more likely to be significant than the particular existing layout, but it is naturally helpful if major work to drains and principal circulations can be avoided. If service ducts or crawlways are present these have to be taken account of in planning alterations.

Extension or demolition

A building which does not immediately appear to be promising for conversion may be viable if a straightforward extension can be added, or subordinate accommodation demolished. In either case, the need to elude the danger of aesthetic damage to the property must be high among the designer's priorities.

Designing the adaptation

The process of design in the case of an alteration must not be thought to be any different in principle from the design of a new building. It is simply the case that as well as the other constraints within which the design has to develop, there are additional parameters imposed by the nature of the building under adaptation.

During the normal stage of determining the priorities to be observed among the established conditions which form the design brief, special thought needs to be given to the relative importance to be accorded to the characteristics of the building as it exists. It may be that conservation of the personality of the building is of the highest importance, though in another case low eventual running costs or the comfort of the occupants, or some other factor, might take precedence.

Arranging the space

A conventional arrangement of the accommodation is frequently impossible in a conversion, and in some cases a less than convenient plan may have to be adopted. A careful balance must be kept between the needs of the occupants and the wish to retain as far as possible the original features of the building. Usually the acceptability of some compromise is implicit in the intention to convert.

The existing spaces may themselves suggest innovative arrangements which will be entirely satisfactory in use: willingness to think laterally is essential. It is necessary to be prepared to escape from commonplace solutions, so that the acceptability of fresh ideas can be objectively assessed.

Where an extension is designed it is often necessary to lose accommodation so as to get reasonable access to the newer wing. This is comparatively unimportant in large buildings, but may be sufficiently significant in smaller ones to render the idea of extension unviable.

For a detailed treatment of design techniques, readers should refer to *Design Procedures IV*, Joan Zunde, Longman Technician Series, 1982.

Improving environmental standards

In most cases the occupants of an adapted building will be readier to accept low lintols and awkward stairs than to tolerate outdated environmental standards. Modern levels of heating, sound and thermal insulation and lighting will generally be expected. The building is unlikely to provide them as it stands, and it may be necessary to devote considerable care to upgrading the building envelope from these points of view.

Heating and thermal insulation

Before considering complete renewal of a heating system it is worthwhile to make an appraisal of the means by which heat is at present escaping from the envelope: this may indicate simple possible improvements which will allow the provision of less capacity than might otherwise seem necessary.

It is very common for significant heat losses from older buildings to occur in any of the following ways, and the building should be examined from this point of view.

Air passages

Draughts through the gaps around doors and windows, gaps between floor boards into ventilated under-floor spaces, and up unused flues can be sufficiently significant to justify the work of draught-stopping. Care should, of course, be taken to leave adequate ventilation, though the opening and closing of doors in the normal use of a building is normally sufficient to ensure the safety of occupants. It is more usual for additional ventilation to be required because of unwanted odours than because oxygen runs low. None the less, where heating by gas, oil or solid fuel is present, the manufacturer's recommendations as to the rate of air flow required must be adhered to. It is also essential to allow some ventilation to closed flues and all spaces containing structural timbers, to obviate the danger of dry rot.

Roof

Heat rises, and an uninsulated roof should in virtually every case be attended to as routine. The addition of roof insulation is simple and comparatively inexpensive, and calculable energy savings are to be anticipated. It is a simple matter to calculate the total heat loss through the existing structure from the conductivities of the materials and the resistances of surfaces of the layers. A comparison can then be made with a second calculation in which the addition of a suitable insulating material is assumed, allowing the saving in heat loss to be demonstrated.

Walls

It is difficult to improve the thermal resistance of wall structures in most cases, though an internal panelling covering insulation and possibly backed with reflective metal foil may be useful. The filling of cavities to existing buildings is hazardous, and should be avoided unless there is a guarantee of success from the installation firm, who agree to correct any consequential damage, and substantial improvements in thermal resistance can be anticipated. The calculations will follow similar lines to those referred to in the case of roofs.

Floor

The addition of an adequate underlay beneath ground-floor carpets will improve insulation. The temptation to apply insulation to the underside of suspended ground-floors should be resisted, as the danger of dry rot exceeds any energy saving that might accrue.

Double-glazing

To be effective in thermal insulation, double-glazing has to be of the sealed type, containing a layer of still air. The units should be designed to avoid a 'cold bridge', and should fit the frames satisfactorily.

Heavy curtain linings may have an almost comparable effect when the curtains are drawn, which is most often the case when temperatures are at their lowest.

In the case of any of these potential improvements to insulation, careful calculations of the anticipated energy saving are essential: unless the capital cost can be made good within about five years, the work is unlikely to be worthwhile. (See Fig. 14.3.)

New heating system

The installation of a new heating system demands consideration of certain aspects which would be less significant in the case of a new building.

Choice of fuel

While the choice of fuel is always one of the most vital decisions in

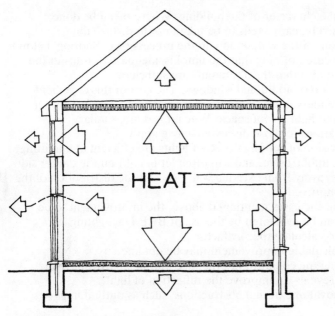

Fig. 14.3 The most economically viable strategies must be adopted to maximise savings on energy

connection with a heating installation, in the case of an existing building the difficulty of providing storage or a suitable flue may constrain the choice.

Pipe runs

If, as is probably the case, no service ducts exists, the design of circulations to cause the least interference with the accommodation can be crucial to the success of the conversion. Vertical runs, in particular, can be difficult to accommodate. A provisional layout of service runs ought to be prepared at an early stage in the development of the scheme for conversion. It may be essential to opt for a particular type of installation (such as storage heating) because it causes little disturbance, while the provision of a ducted warm-air system may be virtually impossible.

Improving natural lighting

The level of natural lighting in older buildings is almost always lower than would be provided in a new one, and improvement may be sought. There are three ways in which this can be achieved.
1. Increasing the size of the windows. This should certainly not be attempted on any important elevation as nothing is more certain to

destroy the character of the building. Where it can be done unobtrusively, care needs to be taken not to disturb the equilibrium of the wall unduly in the process (see 'Shoring' below) and to ensure not only that the lintol is adequate to transfer the loads, but also that the abutments are sufficient.

2. Introduction of additional windows. The cost of this expedient usually renders it uneconomic, excepting in the case of dormer windows to light a roof space. When it is done, similar considerations to those discussed above apply.

3. The provision of roof lights. Roof lights are efficient at admitting daylight, unobtrusive, and will often let in light on the darker side of spaces, away from external walls, so that the distribution of the light is improved.

In each of the cases mentioned above, the improvement to be anticipated can be evaluated by the use of BRE Daylighting Protractors to calculate the sky factor.

A less calculable improvement may be obtained by:

(a) Lightening the colour of internal decorations, particularly to window reveals, to improve the reflection of light.

(b) The removal of external obstructions, such as outbuildings or trees.

(See Fig. 14.4.)

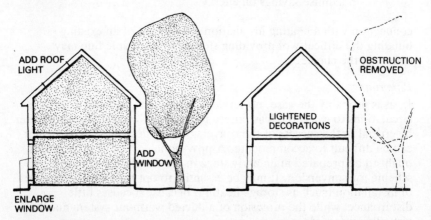

Fig. 14.4 It may not be necessary to increase window area, to improve lighting

Opening-up space

Few older buildings which are available for conversion present the open unobstructed spans which would facilitate adaptation. In many cases a high proportion of the internal walls is loadbearing. A wise rule is to avoid making any opening more than 1.5 m wide and reaching to within 500 mm of the ceiling to structural walls unless every alternative has been explored. This not only preserves much of the original feeling of the building, but ensures that adequate abutments and lintol depths will be available.

Inserting structures

Where the need to insert a structure such as an intermediate floor arises, this should be wherever possible designed as an independent structure, with its own supports, and without the imposition of additional loads, particularly eccentric ones, upon the existing walls. This may imply the desirability of planning larger spaces with clear spans at upper levels, and multi-celled areas below.

Alterations to the structure

The physical dangers of making alterations to existing structures cannot be over-stressed. It is not sufficient to ensure that the completed building will be stable. During construction, both when temporary supports are inserted and when the load is finally transferred to the new structure, careful design and execution are essential.

Shoring

The design of shoring is crucial to such alterations. Shores are of three main types.
1. *Raking shore*. This transfers the weight of an unstable wall to foundations through timbers running at a diagonal angle, and is generally used to support such a structure while investigations into the loss of stability are made.
2. *Flying shore*. In this case the strutting transfers the load to an adjacent building (which it is essential should first be evaluated to ascertain that its own stability will not be jeopardised).
3. *Dead shore*. This is often a steel tubular framework, which is used for temporary support of upper structures during alterations, usually in combination with inserted needles.
(See Fig. 14.5.)
    In each case the load is collected through timber plates, and similarly distributed, and pairs of folding wedges which allow the gradual transfer of the load are essential and critical to success. Temporary adjustable props may offer a useful alternative support.

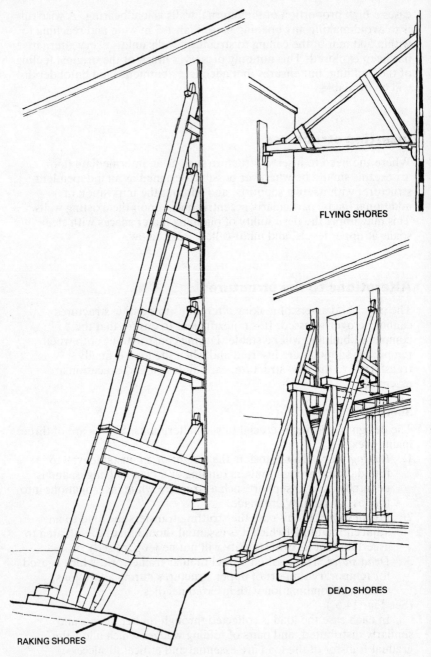

FLYING SHORES

DEAD SHORES

RAKING SHORES

Fig. 14.5 Temporary supports

Extensions

The danger of overloading an existing structure by imposing additional weight from an extension has been mentioned in Chapter 10.

A further point to be borne in mind is the likelihood of differential settlement, or movement due to thermal expansion, at the junction between old and new work. The junction should be designed as an expansion joint for this reason, and in particular care should be taken that no new loads bear on the existing foundations. (See Fig. 14.6.)

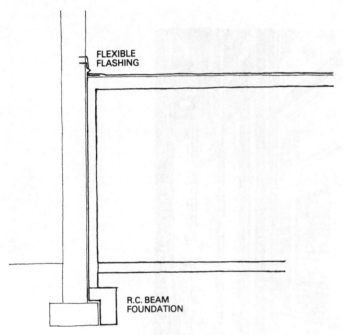

Fig. 14.6 The design of the junction between an extension and the building must allow for movement

Aesthetic problems

It should not be necessary to stress the importance of enhancing the original character of a building when designing alterations rather than making insensitive excursions into inappropriate (though perhaps fashionable) details. This principle should extend to all buildings, no matter how unsympathetic the designer may find their original style. Post Office Georgian or Stockbroker Tudor have to be met with as much empathy as the eighteenth-century Cotswold cottage.

In each case, the features of the original must be analysed so as to establish the genesis of the basic character. The principles of good design then lead the Architect to ensure that the unity of the composition is maintained by the use of similar materials, proportions and motifs, that any extension or introduced window does not destroy (though it may alter) the overall balance, and that the personality of the original is respected. This need not mean – and indeed should not mean – a design in pastiche, but will result in a final design which pays due regard both to the outdated building and to its modern function. (See Fig. 14.7.)

Fig. 14.7 Sympathetic design need not involve pastiche

Listed buildings

A building which is listed as being of historical or architectural importance cannot lightly be altered in any way. Apart from the fact that the planning authority – to say nothing of local conservation groups – would have the strongest and most vocal objections such a course would be totally irresponsible.

One of the major objects of any adaptation is to conserve our endowment of established buildings and the greatest sensitivity is necessary for this to be successfully achieved. Similar considerations apply in the case of conservation areas.

None the less, it has to be admitted that in some areas more buildings are listed than most objective observers would think it necessary to preserve, and planning authorities may be prepared to listen to responsible proposals which suggest more far-reaching alterations than might be at first considered right.

Cost

It is notoriously difficult to estimate in advance the cost of alteration and conversion work, and indeed to control the cost during the course of the contract. A number of methods of achieving these aims have been proposed and tried, with variable success. These are discussed in Chapter 8.

Building for adaptability

The rapidly changing patterns of life and industry in recent decades lead to consideration of other strategies than the provision of carefully tailored one-off buildings. As an alternative to the expense and inconvenience of adapting obsolescent structures to newly established standards and fresh needs it might be appropriate to construct a far higher proportion of buildings as simply adaptable enclosed space. This is, of course, already done in the case of much speculatively-built commercial development. A shell is erected, complete with such services as heating, toilets and lifts, but without partitions, fittings (and often finishes). The tenant subdivides the space to suit his particular needs, and a subsequent occupant expects to be able to gut the building and repeat the operation. (See Fig. 14.8.)

Much such space, while not simply adaptable to such specialised uses as theatres or operating suites, could easily be put to a wide variety of uses.

Offices, light engineering, department stores, schools and many other types of activity have more in common than may appear at first glance. There might be a great deal to be said in favour of providing straightforward framed buildings with a uniform ceiling height, similar standards of heating and light and basic ducted services, which could be readily converted from one such use to another.

It has increasingly been the fashion to design buildings very specifically to suit the precise needs of the users, and this is of course a very desirable and proper aim, and one which must be strongly advocated if optimum efficiency is sought. If one of the conditions understood from the outset was that the accommodation should be readily convertible to some as yet undesignated use the incidence of unwanted white elephants in our cities might be reduced.

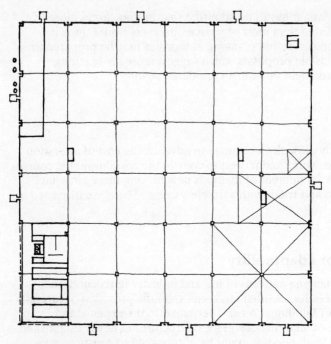

Fig. 14.8 Adaptable space

An alternate strategy is to construct and maintain buildings for a deliberately short life. This was the case with the excellent prefabricated houses put up after the Second World War: this fact reveals the danger of the approach. If the life of such a building should unexpectedly be prolonged, it may be difficult to maintain satisfactorily.

Chapter 15

Factory production

Relationship between design, production and use

A man who sets out to make a platter for his own use has no need of a
specification or drawing. He intends to fulfil a need, whether that is a
practical or a decorative one, selects an appropriate piece of wood, and
'feels' his way to the eventual artefact.

The most primitive buildings are designed and made in just this
way. Improvements are gradually introduced into succeeding
examples, but the builder has no one to please or explain his intentions
to but himself. On the other hand, the extent of his achievement is
limited by his own skill and resources. The typical building is the hut.

In a slightly more sophisticated society more specialisation occurs.
Individual skills are identified and valued, and goods and services are
bartered. A skilled potter makes the utensils everyone will need. He
has to identify not only his own requirements but also those of his
customers, which may be different. There is no argument about the
design because there are no alternatives on offer: what is provided is
self-evidently the most efficient object that could be produced for its
purpose in the local circumstances and using the available materials.
Since the community is small, competition is unlikely.

At this stage of development, the building-owner is at once remove
from its design: the local builder, however, uses the local materials in
an established and accepted way. The village is the unit of design, and
the typical dwelling is the cottage. (See Fig. 15.1.)

Fig. 15.1 Specialised skills adopted locally

As communications improve, communities become larger and competition in price and quality develops. The advantages of employing a skilled designer to devise (say) a suit of clothes becomes apparent. He has the knowledge to advise on the selection from a wide range of possibilities, and can balance the factors of cost and quality.

Similarly, diversity in the kinds of buildings available increases. Materials can be brought from a distance and used in a variety of ways. An Architect is employed to advise the building-owner on getting the building he needs from this plethora of possibilities.

The designer further distances the building-owner from the building of his shelter, but pays close attention to the owner's individual needs. The overall concept of the unity of the town may be lost, and the typical dwelling is the house.

Subsequently, society becomes industrialised, and the owners and the users of buildings become separated. A stage in which profitability may seem more important than convenience is discernible. Entrepreneurs arrange for the production of those goods from which they can anticipate the fastest and greatest profit, and the consumer chooses from a range of goods offered to him. This is likely to be heavily weighted towards those goods thought likely to be reasonably satisfactory in the majority of circumstances, and so to satisfy most of the market at a reasonable price. At the other extreme there will be expensive specialised goods which are less attractive commercially: these are not necessarily luxury items – it is dearer and more difficult to buy unusual sizes of clothing than 'average' sizes. The speculative estate is typical of the first of these alternatives, while an individually designed house, tailor made for its occupants but not necessarily more spacious, is typical of the second.

Later there is a tendency towards increasing authoritarianism. As in medicine, the knowledge of the specialist so far outstrips that of the layman that the latter has little alternative to passive acceptance of the advice offered. 'They' know what is best for him. So far as houses are concerned an ever-increasing brigade of experts – economists, sociologists, planners, housing managers . . . produce well-meant advice, which yet farther distances a man from the design of his living space. He typically must accept 'housing'. This has one advantage, though: there is a return to the town, or at least the estate, as the unit of design.

Where Western society is concerned this is, on the whole, the position today, in building.

In the case of many other commodities, a very wide range of goods is offered, between which a consumer can choose. He may be unaware of any influence on the initial design process, but he is, in fact, very powerful. Only a design which satisfies his needs and prejudices, and those of his fellows, can be commercially viable.

This brings him closer to the design process than he has been for many generations. His ability to choose between a wide range of factory-made goods in a store or from a catalogue gives him power over the designer. The operation of this mechanism is clearly seen in the marketing of motor cars.

Where buildings are concerned, the increasing factory design and manufacture of components should lead to a similar position, though this has yet to be observed. Certainly, there is little reason for pessimism because of a perceived decline in 'craftsmanship' due to jobs being transferred to the factory. As has been traced in this very simplified description of the evolution of industrialisation, the process has been a gradual one over many generations, based on the use of those with specialised skills to perform the tasks at which they excel.

Design for the factory

The design of factory-made components is not based upon the same considerations as that of the tailor-made, specifically devised article. It is subject to commercial pressures. The most important difference is that the decision to produce the object is based on a belief that it will be profitable rather than on a perceived need. Clearly, the product will fail to sell if no market exists, but the need which is rarest and most difficult to fulfil is likely to be excluded from the manufacturer's consideration.

The objectives of the manufacturer, and therefore of his designer, will include the following four factors concerning profitability, employment, and the product itself.

Profitability
1.   He will identify a gap in the market which he can fill, on the basis

of perhaps quite extensive market research. This will be coupled with a need to maximise his sales, so he will subsequently advertise extensively to draw the attention of his potential customers to the fine qualities of the goods he has to offer – and often, too, to the hitherto unperceived need they have of these goods.

He must seek to establish and maintain a reputation for quality, or service, or economy, or response to fashion (but not necessarily all of those qualities) which will improve his sales.

Should he be a mere opportunist, however, he may simply be looking for a high initial profit without any wish to maintain a market, and huckstering alone will serve his purpose.

2. It will be important to him to make the fullest use of his plant, whether this is plant he already has or he intends to equip a works specially. Such plant will have a defined economic life, over which the capital cost is spread (in the way discussed in Ch. 8). The plant will, too, have a limited degree of adaptability: the more automated it is, and so the more sophisticated, the truer this may be.

3. Continuous production runs are generally considered to be crucial to commercial success. The percentage of time during which a particular plant will be out of action, for maintenance, for re-tooling, or because orders are intermittent, will have been established as an important component in evaluating the viability of the enterprise. Unless continuity of production can be assured the project is unlikely to be attractive to the investor. He is therefore most likely to concentrate on a perceived mass-market.

4. One important advantage of factory production, which must not be lost, is that it exploits unskilled labour to the maximum extent. Each process must be broken down into a series of very simple stages if this is to be achieved.

Employment

A further aim of an enlightened employer will be to provide work in an area where this is needed and to maintain continuity of employment. He will wish for a mutually beneficial relationship with his workforce.

Product

Low on the manufacturer's list of objectives, but none the less present there, will be the provision of a safe, useful product. Since this is, in itself, its own best advertisement, it is an aspect of his operations which he neglects at his peril.

Selection of manufactured goods

An increasing proportion of the design process in building is concerned with the selection of goods and components designed and made commercially. It is unfortunately true that such choices are sometimes made with insufficient consideration; the designer should make a careful and critical assessment of a potential choice, remembering:

(a) The commercial motivation of the manufacturer.
(b) The function of advertising to increase sales and maintain demand, and not necessarily to inform.
(c) The importance of unity in any overall design. Parts culled from a variety of sources may be admirable in themselves and yet so diverse as to disrupt the overall concept. It is this consideration which leads to the special design of components and fittings for the most prestigious projects.

Systems building

One advantage of choice of a constructional system should be the unity which this automatically imposes on the concept. There has been considerable emphasis on the development of entire building systems, where the larger part of the components will have been specifically designed to be compatible. They are also, of course, usually designed so that the parts needed can be obtained only from a single source, so that a captive market is created. The choice of such a system, just as much as the choice of a single component, must be made in awareness of the considerations outlined above.

Advantages of systems building

Three major advantages are sometimes claimed for systems building.

Cost

While mass-production in many other industries leads to economy, this has yet to be demonstrated in the case of buildings. This is probably due to the lack of the very large market that would make economies of scale feasible.

Speed

While site erection is usually fast, the period between initiation of the project and occupation is little reduced in actual experience. The period on site may be important in some cases, but excepting where manufacturers can actually store completed components it seems unlikely that the overall project period can be significantly reduced. It should be noted that conventional building can be speeded-up very considerably, providing the cost disadvantages can be considered unimportant.

Quality

It is usually reasonable to expect a more consistent standard of quality where work is carried out under controlled factory conditions.

These three considerations are further discussed below (see p. 194).

Systems can be considered, in the main, under two important groupings.

Closed systems

This term, in the present context, implies a series of manufactured parts which can be put together in a single order to produce a predetermined end-result, as might be the case with a motor car. This is designed in detail before manufacture is much considered. Examples of buildings designed in this way include site offices and simple dwellings. (See Fig. 15.2.) The total building has to be broken-down into a series of elements of a suitable size to transport and handle on site, but apart from this can be fully assembled in the factory, even to services and finishes. A foundation and site services generally have to be provided in the traditional way.

Fig. 15.2 Building in a closed system

Open systems

Open systems are those which consist of a kit of parts which are designed to be assembled in a wide variety of different ways. (See Fig. 15.3.)

Although such a system would be difficult to develop unless the designers had a clear idea of the needs of a particular building type in terms of spans and ceiling heights and levels of natural lighting and so on, this need not constrain the imagination of the Architect, who

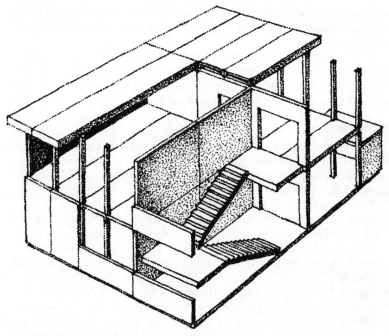

Fig. 15.3 Building with an open system

should find the options available to him no less wide than they would be with any other form of construction. He will, however, find two important differences from traditional construction:

1. Assembly will usually be 'dry' with the joints depending for their effectiveness on gaskets and interlocking devices (this is also true of a 'closed' system).
2. Modular coordination will be critical: if the parts are to be interchangeable so that a wide range of end-results is possible, it is essential that all-over dimensional discipline should be established. This must be accepted by the designer, as otherwise he will lose the advantages for which the system was presumably chosen.

Design of a prefabricated system

The design of a prefabricated system will start on the basis described above for any factory-made object. That is to say, there will be important commercial considerations, and no manufacturer would proceed with development unless he was assured of maximum use of his plant, adequate profitability and so on.

There have, however, been a number of systems developed

cooperatively by manufacturers, contractors and potential users (such as education authorities) and Architects with a specific programme of buildings in view.

In any case, an early decision will revolve around the particular types of buildings – commercial, domestic, educational, for example – to be aimed for. This will dictate the number of floors, maximum floor loadings, spans, types of cladding and so on.

Objectives

It is also crucial that the design team should be clear about the reasons for adopting system building, since these may vary, and some of the claimed advantages may be incompatible with others. The objectives will affect many of their choices.

Possible objectives might include

(a) *Cost*. An appreciable financial advantage will in practice only be obtained if very long assured runs of repetitive components can be arranged. If cost saving is vital it may be essential to limit the range of options available, even to the point of designing a closed system.

(b) *Speed*. Where speed is important, as it might be in the rapid provision of emergency housing, there must be either a continuous production line, like that for a car, or the bulk of the detailed work must be in the preparation of jigs or moulds which can be stored to be quickly put into use when a need arises. Fibreglass or concrete components might lend themselves to such techniques.

(c) *Quality*. One major advantage of factory production is ease of supervision, which along with the controlled working conditions provided can lead to high and uniform quality of production. If, however, either speed or cheapness is vital, a compromise may have to be made in this respect.

(d) *Use of unskilled labour*. Factory production is much less voracious of skilled labour than work on site. In the case of a developing country this could be an important indicator to the choice of prefabrication. In other circumstances, the degree of automation available might be an important consideration.

Materials

In some cases there is a prerequisite that a particular material is to be employed. The manufacturer's expertise and the skills of his workforce, the plant he wishes to utilise, or his supply of raw materials, may predetermine the major structural choices. In other instances it may be possible to make a comparative evaluation to select materials.

In either case, it is then necessary to survey the manufacturing methods generally adopted with the chosen material (and possibly less conventional ones as well) to understand their scope and limitations, and to appreciate the implications of particular constructional decisions.

Function

In parallel with this investigation, study of the optimum functioning of the components, so that a performance specification can be prepared for each one, must be made. This will provide parameters for strength, weight, size, thermal properties and so on. Handling and transport and the ability of the assembled component to bear its own weight during site handling will be considered as well as the function of the component throughout the life of the building.

Jointing

A system depends upon the excellence of the jointing techniques adopted. The joints are the most vulnerable and critical part of the fabric, and must be designed to allow for:

(a) Adequate tolerances to cover inaccuracies of manufacture and of setting-out on site.
(b) Ease of site assembly, taking account of the order in which the parts will be put together.
(c) Potential movement due to changes of temperature, wind-loading and use.
(d) The need to maintain weatherproofing (including thermal resistance) during movement and at the extreme tolerances.
(e) Fatigue.
(f) Ease of repair and replacement. (See Fig. 15.4.)

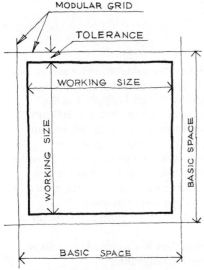

Fig. 15.4 Jointing tolerances

Grid

It will emerge at this stage that, on functional as well as constructional
grounds, a particular planning and constructional grid is to be
preferred. (See Fig. 15.5.)

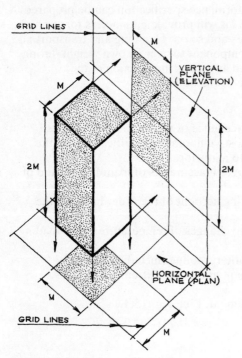

GRID LINES

M

VERTICAL
PLANE
(ELEVATION)

2M

2M

HORIZONTAL
PLANE (PLAN)

M

GRID LINES

M

Fig. 15.5 Planning grid

This may well be related to optimum manufacturing sizes, the sizes
in which raw materials are delivered, and to functional components,
such as doorway widths. Very commonly the grid adopted in this
country is 1 m square on plan and section, subdivided into 100 mm
substeps. For housing planning and construction, the major module
may be 900 mm. In either case, not every 100 mm step will be
adopted, but the preferred dimensions will be related to the particular
demands of the building type and materials, so as to allow for
thicknesses of components and reasonable increments of room size. It
is unusual to allow floor planning to adopt a split module.

The grid may be designed to lie either at the centre of structural
components or to surround them.

The adoption of a grid for an open (but not a closed) system is
essential if the parts are to be truly interchangeable.

Parts

Individual components can next be designed to fulfil the requirements of the performance specifications and to employ the jointing technique devised. The aim should always be to limit the range of available options as rigorously as possible, especially in the case of those components from whose manufacture the greatest advantages of series production are expected. Every alternative proposed must be stringently evaluated to establish that it in fact fulfils an identified need (which may, of course, be simply to provide variety of appearance) and that it does this as simply as possible.

Building design

The design of the actual building follows. In the general run it is essential that the constraints imposed by the system – dimensional, choice of materials and so on – are fully accepted by the Architect. However, the first few projects designed in a new system are likely to be in part developmental projects and may lead, quite properly, to modifications in the system itself.

Non factory-made systems

Some firms of builders offer constructional systems, of which they have experience and skill, from which they will produce buildings by largely traditional methods. Such systems depend on the repetition of standard details for their success and are often not based upon dry construction. They share the disadvantage of limited tendering competition with manufacturers' systems, and impose no less stringent discipline upon the designer.

Tendering

The only practicable way to ensure some competition in the tendering for buildings to be based on a system is to invite tenders on an outline sketch scheme and detailed performance specification and to redesign in detail when the system to be adopted has been selected. This may neutralise some of the advantages supposed to be obtained from the use of a system.

Designers' systems

An extension of the notion of standard details may lead to the adoption by a practice or an authority of what is virtually its own 'system' of building. This is very much what occurred in earlier periods throughout the industry, when a well-understood 'vernacular' of design was applied, or even where sophisticated classical details were adopted. Many of the advantages of systems building can be obtained, without the disadvantages of dry construction, lack of competitive tendering, or transport costs and difficulties.

Advantages

It is desirable to enquire what advantages are expected from the adoption of a system and to whom.

As has been seen, it is clearly to the advantage of a manufacturer to devise a satisfactory and widely adopted system, though he takes a very considerable commercial risk in deciding to proceed. Once he is in production it is very important to him to maintain continuity, as discussed above, and this factor should ensure consistent quality and acceptable price in spite of his powerful monopoly position.

A designer will find the use of a system convenient and labour saving: only layout drawings need be prepared for the superstructure, since the manufacturer's detail drawings already exist. Some designers find the constraints upon their imagination constricting, though with a well devised system this should not be the case. Any material or form of construction imposes constraints, and those presented by a system should not be more irksome simply because they are unfamiliar.

The client may hope to save money, which is only likely if he accepts a completely standardised building. He may expect to save time, although from initiation of the project to occupation this is uncommon. Actual time on site may well be saved, which can be important in some circumstances, but allowing for manufacture and delivery the overall saving is usually minimal. Time-saving on site is a function of meticulous pre-planning and incurs financial penalties. This is nearly as important with traditional as with system construction.

Because the appearance of system buildings is less familiar than the traditional type, these tend to be unpopular with the public. Everyone likes what is familiar. The appearance of systems buildings can be satisfactorily attractive and well disciplined because of the unifying effect of the constraints of the system. The materials are often the same as those used in traditional building, excepting that brick is comparatively rare.

The quality of the thought devoted to the development of non-traditional constructional systems is high. If comparable study was made of traditional methods, and the design of buildings using them was as carefully considered, especially in the adoption of a three-dimensional planning and constructional grid, it might well be that equivalent advantages to those attributed to system construction might be obtained, without the disadvantages.

Index